The Best of
CLOVIS G. CHAPPELL

The Best of
CLOVIS G. CHAPPELL

Compiled by
Cornelius Zylstra

BAKER BOOK HOUSE
Grand Rapids, Michigan 49506

Copyright 1984 by
Baker Book House Company

ISBN: 0-8010-2500-1

Sermons 1 and 2 originally appeared in *Sermons from Revelation*. Copyright renewal © 1970 by Clovis G. Chappell. Used with permission of Abingdon Press.

Sermons 4, 5, and 6 originally appeared in *Chappell's Special Day Sermons*. Copyright renewal © 1963 by Clovis G. Chappell. Used with permission of Abingdon Press.

Sermon 14 originally appeared in *Sermons from the Parables*. Copyright renewal © 1961 by Clovis G. Chappell. Used with permission of Abingdon Press.

Sermon 20 originally appeared in *Feminine Faces*. Copyright renewal © 1969 by Clovis G. Chappell. Used with permission of Abingdon Press.

PHOTOLITHOPRINTED BY CUSHING - MALLOY, INC.
ANN ARBOR, MICHIGAN, UNITED STATES OF AMERICA

Contents

1. The Cold Church   7
   (Rev. 2:4)

2. The Rich Church   15
   (Rev. 2:9)

3. The Unfinished Sermon   23
   (Acts 24:25)

4. Mother Ostrich (Mother's Day)   32
   (Lam. 4:3)

5. A Father's Failure (Father's Day)   40
   (2 Sam. 18:33)

6. The Work of the Evangelist   48
   (2 Tim. 4:5)

7. Poverty that Makes Rich   56
   (Matt. 5:3)

8. The Peacemakers   64
   (Matt. 5:9)

9. The First Word from the Cross   73
   (Luke 23:34)

10. The Seventh Word from the Cross   80
    (Luke 23:46)

11. God's Plan for My Life   87
    (John 17:4)

12. The Forks of the Road—Moses   97
    (Heb. 11:24-26)

13 The Beloved Physician—Luke   105
    (2 Tim. 4:11)

14 The Quest for the Best   114
    (Matt. 13:45,46)

15 Perpetual Thanksgiving—Paul   123
    (1 Thess. 5:18)

16 The Supreme Question—The Philippian Jailer   133
    (Acts 16:30,31)

17 I'd Avoid Being Half-Baked   141
    (Hos. 7:8)

18 That Fox—Herod   150
    (Luke 13:32)

19 The Fatal Refusal   159
    (Mark 10:22)

20 The Frozen Face—Lot's Wife   166
    (Gen. 19:26)

1
The Cold Church

I have this against thee, that thou didst leave thy first love (Rev. 2:4, ARV).

The Book of Revelation is in a sense an Epistle addressed to the Church of that day. The seven letters contained in chapters two and three are therefore letters within a letter. The first of these is addressed to the church at Ephesus. Ephesus was at that time a great and thriving city. It was a cosmopolitan city of rich and poor, of cultured and ignorant, of artisans and merchants. Here was the famous temple of Diana, one of the seven wonders of the ancient world. The city derived much of its wealth from the manufacture and sale of images of this goddess. Here paganism was strong, seasoned, and respectable.

Into this wicked and idolatrous city came the heralds of the Cross. Among them was the eloquent, gifted, but imperfectly instructed Apollos. Timid Timothy had preached here; also John, the Beloved Apostle. Tradition says that these two, along with the Virgin Mary, are buried here. Here no doubt had preached the author of this book. But the church owed most to Paul, the ablest and the hottest heart of them all. He had preached here for nearly three years. Under his leadership the church had become an institution of power both in the city and in the surrounding country. It was to the official board of this church that Paul gave that marvelous address recorded in the twentieth chapter of the Book of Acts. In it he urged them to watchfulness and warned them of the wolves that would one day threaten their flock.

Since the giving of that warning, more than a quarter century has passed. Today, John, speaking by inspiration of his Risen Lord, is sending this letter. It begins with a note of authority. The Christ in whose name he writes qualifies as an expert. He speaks as one who knows: "To the angel of the church in Ephesus write: These things saith he that holdeth the seven stars in his right hand, he that walketh in the midst of the seven golden lampstands: I know. . . ."

I

What does John, speaking in behalf of Christ, know about this church? He knows much that is good. It would fairly make our hearts sing to hear such commendations of the church of which we are a part.

A. "I know thy works," he declares. "I know the difference that your presence in that city has made. I know the beneficent changes that you have wrought in the hearts of individuals, in the homes of the people, in all human relationships. I know the shattered and broken lives that you have remade. I know how you have changed despair into hope, and hate into love." In the Book of Acts we read of a riot in this city that was brought about by those interested in the image trade. This church had so successfully brought to the people of Ephesus the living Christ that many of them had thrown away their images of Diana, while others were refusing to buy. Thus the evil of idolatry was being swept away. The presence of this church was making a difference.

"I know thy works." Our Master can say the same about every living church today. The church whose presence in the city fails to make that city better is a dead church. "I know thy works"—that word our Lord ought to be able to say, not only to every church, but to every member of the church. Can he say it about you and me? What is there of good in our church, what is there of good in our city, or in our world, that simply could not be there but for the fact of our presence? If there is nothing, then our Christianity is a sheer futility. Every living church, every living Christian, is accomplishing something. Where these farm, the wheat fields grow golden and ripe for harvest.

Not only does every living church have to its credit some

positive good; it also accomplishes other results that often none sees but God. For the presence of a vigorous church in a community not only accomplishes worthwhile tasks, but makes many an evil impossible. This is the type of achievement that can never get into our reports. Granting that our members are faulty, granting that many an evil still stalks unafraid in our presence, yet this we need to bear in mind—the situation would be far worse if we were not here. As Christians, we are the salt of the earth. We not only remake broken lives; we keep many a life from being broken. This was what the church at Ephesus was doing. Therefore John, speaking for his Lord, could say, "I know thy works."

B. "I know thy toil." That is, "I know the effort, the sacrifices, the struggles that have been necessary in order for you to accomplish the tasks that you have accomplished." This church at Ephesus has not dreamed its way to great achievements. Its accomplishments have been at the price of strenuous and sacrificial effort. These saints have been able to bless because they have been willing to bleed. That is ever the case. Nothing worthwhile is accomplished in any field except at the price of hard work. Wherever there is an abundant harvest, it has come at the price of somebody's toil. We do not expect to win in any field of endeavor without work. At least there seems to be only one exception, and that is in the field of religion. So often we seem to fancy that here we ought to make vast progress, without any effort whatever!

"I know thy toil." I wonder if the Master can say that about you and me. Many of us take our church membership far too lightly. For some the cost is naked nothing. To such it is worth exactly what it cost, and that only. One day the Master saw a great crowd that to our gaze might have looked like so many happy folks on a picnic. But he saw them as they really were. Therefore they reminded him of sheep without a shepherd. He not only saw these people as they were; he saw also the amazing possibilities that were locked in them. Therefore he said, "Pray ye the Lord of the harvest, that he would thrust forth labourers into his harvest." That is the need of this hour, and of every hour. We have enough drones, enough idlers, enough good people who are at ease in Zion. What we need is laborers, men and women of whom Jesus can say, "I know thy toil, and I know the works that are the result of this toil. I know beautiful deeds that are blossoming like flowers all over your city that would be impossible but for you."

C. "I know your zeal for the truth, your sincere and intelligent orthodoxy. You have tried them who say they are apostles and are not, and have found them false." These people had been instructed by some of the greatest teachers of the Early Church. They knew what they believed and why. In the light of this teaching, they tested the traveling preachers that came their way. If they found them speaking what was not according to sound doctrine, they rejected them. That was wise. Too many of our professing Christians know neither what they believe nor why.

D. Not only did these people have a zeal for right doctrine, not only did they reject false teachers, but they rejected also those whose lives did not ring true. They were commended because they could not endure evil men. They refused to have fellowship in the church with open and flagrant sinners. There was a time, even in recent years, when those whose lives were a discredit to the church were expelled. I am not saying that this was the best method. I am quite sure that it was not. Jesus had a renegade by the name of Judas in his group, but he refused to turn him out. He knew that if love and patience could not save him, expulsion would be sure to fail. But even expulsion, faulty as it is, might be better than the attitude of indifference that often characterizes us. These people had such a genuine zeal for right living that they refused to tolerate evil men.

E. "I know thy patience." Patience seems to have been an outstanding characteristic of this church. It is mentioned more than once. Its membership had been patient under opposition, patient under persecution. When days were sunny, they could be counted on. When days were cloudy, they could be counted on nonetheless. When the church was prospering and going from victory to victory, they were there. When sore trials came and they seemed faced with disaster and defeat, they still stood by. "You are enduring patiently and have borne up for my sake and have not wearied."

What a church this was! Had this letter, written by one who could speak with authority, come to me regarding my own church, the first part of it would have brought great joy. I think I might have left off when I had read these words of commendation to give a shout of real enthusiasm. The church was working patiently. It was accomplishing something. It was seeking to be Christian both in doctrine and in life. Surely, we feel, this leaves little else to be desired. What more could one ask of any church? Yet, there was something wrong. Having said all these lovely things, the author passes on to his one adverse criticism.

II

What is that criticism? "I have this against thee, that thou didst leave thy first love." "Yet I have this against you," Weymouth translates it, "that you no longer love Me as you did at first." "But I have this against you," Moffatt translates it; "you have given up loving one another as you did at first." All these translations are correct. This church was still active and earnest. It was decent, respectable, and orthodox. Its one fault was that it was failing in its love for Christ and, therefore, for one another. It was losing its glow and its zest, its fire and enthusiasm. It was growing cold, and about the most tragic thing in all the world is a cold church.

"I have this against thee, that thou didst leave thy first love." First love is the love of espousal. It is the love of the honeymoon days. Sad to say, the honeymoon for many married couples is an exceedingly brief period. It is over almost as quickly as the wedding tour. How soon, for many, the radiance and romance fade into the dull, drab commonplace! If you have been married as long as twenty years and do not love each other better than you did in the honeymoon days, the chances are that you love each other far less. And if you do not love Christ more today than when you first met him, you are on the way to ceasing to love him altogether. In spite, therefore, of all that was commendable in this live and active church, there remained this pathetic fact that the warm springtime of love was slowly changing into winter.

Just why this change was taking place, we are not told. But as we read between the lines, I think we can make a fairly accurate guess. The coldness was the result of something that was in its beginning commendable. At first these Christians had contended earnestly for the faith because of their love for the truth and of their hatred of error. But it is very hard persistently to contend with some misguided brother without growing a bit proud and critical and pharisaical. It is well enough to contend, provided we can do so in a spirit of love. But how easy it is for the contender to come to damn everybody who does not agree with him! Every heresy-hunter is in great danger of losing his first love if he has not already lost it before he begins his unedifying task. "Better that error live than that love should die."

III

What is the tragedy of the cold church?

A. It is lacking in winsomeness. What is the most attractive characteristic that either a church or an individual can possess? It is love for others. The Early Church, because of its warmth of heart, breathed on the world of that day like a spiritual springtime. "How these Christians love each other!" the amazed pagans exclaimed. They watched the Christians as they entertained strangers and declared that they even loved folks they had never seen. And sometimes when pestilence was abroad and these pagans would turn their own loved ones out to die, they were awed and astounded to see the Christians take them to their homes and to their hearts. It was the love of the Early Church that made the desert to rejoice and to blossom as a rose.

In recent years a book entitled *How to Win Friends and Influence People* has been popular. There is much sound sense in the book; there is also much sound selfishness. But the author is right in teaching that friendliness begets friends. If you feel lonely and unfriended, if you deeply yearn for the joy of human love, there is a roadway to this treasure that the weakest and the most handicapped can find. In order to be loved, it is not necessary to be either beautiful, or gifted, or young. There is just one necessity, and that is to love. Love begets love as certainly as night follows day. The church or the individual, therefore, that has grown cold has lost the supreme secret of winsomeness.

B. Not only does a loveless church cease to be attractive; it also finally ceases to be active. This cold church was still working; it still had worthwhile deeds to its credit but it was going ahead largely upon the momentum of the past. Sometime ago I was out driving, and my car ran out of gasoline. But it did not stop the very instant the tank was empty. It ran for a little while under the momentum that it had gathered while there was power. But soon the wheels would not turn another time. The church that has lost its first love may be active for a while, but soon its activities will cease. One reason there are so many idlers in the church is that many have ceased to care.

C. The final tragedy of the cold church is that not only is it lacking in winning power and in effort, but it is on its way to certain death. All that is necessary in order for the individual Christian to die is to do nothing. The same is true of a church. How long will our church live? Just so long as its membership cares enough to carry on its work! Therefore Jesus warned that unless these recovered their first love he would move the lampstand out of its place. This does not mean that in anger he will come in judgment. It only means that the loveless church will die a natural death. The church cannot live except as it loves.

IV

Is there any hope for this church that is growing cold? There is. It is because of this hope that this letter was written. The author tells us that in order to pass from winter into springtime only three steps are necessary.

A. "Remember whence thou art fallen." To cease to love is always to fall. Jesus comes, therefore, to these who have thus fallen and seeks to call to their minds those great yesterdays when their hearts were warm. "Remember," he says. How beautifully tender! He is appealing to them by the memories of the best that they have known. It is thus that one loving human heart which has been wounded might appeal to another. Here, for instance, is a wife who has been made to realize that there is a widening chasm between her and the husband she loves. For years they have lived joyfully together. But now there is coldness where once there was warmth, indifference where there was once glowing love. How naturally would she appeal to him by the memories of those gracious days that had dropped into the sunset! "Remember," she would say, "how we have laughed together, and how also we have wept! Remember the comfort and courage of our mutual helpfulness in love's bright morning long ago."

Thus Jesus appeals to this church, and to you and to me: "Remember whence thou art fallen. Remember that great hour when you first met me. Remember those better days when you could sing with reality, 'Blessed assurance, Jesus is mine!' Remember how I have been your comfort in the hours of grief, your companion in hours of loneliness. Remember how I have been your stay in the night watches, and your morning and sunrise at the breaking of day. There was a time when you sang zestfully, 'I was glad when they said unto me, let us go into the house of the Lord.' There was a time when for love's sake you labored for a better world. Remember whence thou art fallen."

B. "Repent." This cold church needs to repent even as you and I. Of what are we to repent? We, as this church, are to repent of our lack of love. The purpose of remembering is to lead to repentance. When the prodigal was away in the far country, it was the memory of his better days that made it impossible for him to stay there. He was haunted by home scenes and home voices. He could not brush out of his mind the memory of the kindest face into which he had ever looked, and the tenderest heart that he had known—that of his father. At last he could endure it no longer. These tormenting and heartening memories so pressed upon him that he said, "I will arise and go to my father."

C. "Do the first works." That is, "Act as you did at first." This is to be the outcome of repentance. To repent is to change one's mind. It is such a change of mind as to lead to a change of conduct. It was not enough for the prodigal to realize his own hunger. It was not enough for him to be gripped by homesickness for his father. His repentance was complete only when he turned his steps home and kept going till he felt the kiss of his father's lips and the hug of his father's arms. It was this that the memory of her better days was to do for this church. Maybe you too have lost the glow out of your life. Maybe your heart has grown cold. Then let the memories of your better days lead you to turn your steps to where Love is waiting to forgive and to forget. "Remember whence thou art fallen, and repent and act as you did at first." Doing this, your winter will surely change into spring.

2
The Rich Church

But thou art rich (Rev. 2:9).

Just forty miles from the city of Ephesus stood and still stands the city of Smyrna. Of all the seven cities it alone is of any importance today. The others have gone into utter eclipse. Smyrna was a progressive and prosperous city. It was inhabited very largely by Jews. These Jews were exceedingly friendly to Rome. It would seem that they were chiefly interested in material wealth. They were eager to stay on friendly terms with the powers that be. Hence, they with their fellow citizens had built a statue to the Roman Emperor Tiberius. These Jews were especially antagonistic to Christianity. The first persecution suffered by this church was at the hands of Jews. Rome continued their cruel work a few years later. Here still is pointed out the tomb of the beloved bishop of this church, Polycarp, who died a martyr to his faith in the year 155.

I

It is to this hard-pressed church that John is sending a letter on behalf of his Master. In the midst of this letter he pays this church, by way of parenthesis, a great compliment. He says of it, "Thou art rich." That is a word of commendation to quicken interest. It tends to lay firm hands upon our sluggish minds and to shake them into wakefulness. The more worldly we are, the more thrilling that word becomes, especially if we fail to understand the nature of the wealth of which the author is speaking. "Thou art rich." What happy pictures that suggests! At once we see a lovely building. There are beautiful pews, comfortably cushioned. There is exquisite music. There is a scholarly and able minister. There is a well-dressed congregation. Here is a church that can not only minister to our religious needs, but also help us incidentally toward the realization of our social and economic ambitions. "But thou art rich."

The phrase has a pleasing sound even to some of us who are in the ministry. Sometime ago a rather worldly and cynical woman was telling me of attending an evening service at a well-known city church. She declared that the pastor apologized to her at the close of the service for both the quality and quantity of his congregation. "You ought to have been here this morning," he said regretfully. "We have a whole pew full of millionaires in the morning. We call it 'Millionaire's Row.' But my best people do not attend in the evening." If attending one service a day is a mark of spiritual aristocracy, not to attend at all ought to rank one as belonging to royalty.

Not only is John's statement an arresting compliment, but it is also unique. There is no other church in the New Testament that is described as being rich. There is one other that thought of itself as rich. That was the lukewarm church in Laodicea. Here is what it thought of itself: "I am rich, and increased with goods, and have need of nothing." But here is the startling truth as Jesus saw it: "If there is a pitiable one it is you, wretched, and miserable, and poor, and blind, and naked."

That is, this church was not in reality rich at all. Of course it was rich in things. But that is not enough. A rich church is to be prized, provided it is rich in values other than money. The Bible has no war to make against money in itself. Money is power. A consecrated rich man can render a greater service, other things being equal, than a consecrated poor man. This is the case because a million dollars dedicated to God can do more than a dedicated penny. A rich man who is also a good man can be a great asset, but a rich man who is self-centered and grasping can be a great liability. This church at Laodicea, being rich only in things, was in reality poverty-stricken. It was suffering from delusions of grandeur.

Some years ago while holding a meeting in the capital of

another state, I became friendly with a fine Christian physician who was superintendent of the state hospital. He invited me to sit in on some of his clinics. Among those who came before us was a fine-looking chap who had a sense of well-being written in every line of his face. "What do you do?" asked the physician. "I am a businessman," came the proud reply. "I own all the national banks in the United States and half of the post offices." "My!" said the physician, "You must work a great many men." "I do," came the answer. "Henry Ford works for me. Old Man John D. Rockefeller used to work for me." But when the physician offered him a quarter, he accepted it eagerly. "Why did you accept that money," someone questioned him, "if you are so rich?" "I did not wish to hurt the doctor's feelings," was the prompt reply. I think I have never met a rich man who enjoyed his wealth any more.

Not only is this an exciting and unique compliment, but it is in a sense all-inclusive. The Master had some lovely words of commendation for the church at Ephesus. But there was also one bit of adverse criticism. "I have this against thee, that thou didst leave thy first love." But with this church he has no fault to find. By this we are not to understand that the church was absolutely perfect. It had not completely arrived, but it was on its way. It was increasingly becoming a glorious church without spot or blemish. When, therefore, the Master said, "Thou art rich," he was saying about the best that could be said. This commendation was gripping, unique, and all-inclusive.

II

Wherein was it rich? Of course, it was rich because of certain assets, but it was also rich in spite of certain liabilities. We are always rich, if at all, *in spite of* as well as *because of*. Look at some of the liabilities of this church. I do not name them in the order used by John.

A. It was a slandered church. "I know the blasphemy." A better translation of the word is *"slander."* This church was ringed about by foes. These foes were giving themselves the luxury of being harshly critical. They were tearing the reputation of this church into shreds by saying all manner of evil against it falsely. The more they criticized, the more they hated.

And the more they hated, the more they criticized. It is possible for us to talk ourselves into hating the best friend we have in the world. This church, then, was being slandered.

B. Not only was it being slandered, but it was being persecuted. The persecution was the natural outcome of the slander. When Rome burned, the Christians were accused of burning it. The accusation was false. It was a slander, but it led to opposition and to bitter persecution. It caused hundreds to be fed to the lions or to be hanged upon forests of crosses. The persecution against this church at Smyrna had not gone quite so far yet, but it had had two results. These slanderers had perhaps incited mobs that had gone about despoiling the shops and the homes of these Christians. It is amazing how much more cruel a mob is than the individuals that compose it. Many a man in a mob will do evil deeds that he would never think of doing if he were alone. These people were being pillaged and plundered somewhat as the Jews have been pillaged and plundered in Nazi Germany. Not only were they thus robbed of their goods, but they were also robbed of an opportunity to work. Men were thrown out of position. Trade-unions would not employ them.

C. This led to a third tragic liability. The membership of this church was reduced to poverty. "I know," says the author, "thy poverty." "Poverty" here is a strong word. It means beggary. These people had been reduced to utter want. The wolf was howling at the door. If they had a pastor, they could keep him only by his being willing to share their poverty with them. They did not have enough between them to buy a half-dozen songbooks. Slandered, persecuted, they had been reduced to dire poverty.

D. Finally, the worst is yet to come. After the author has named these liabilities, we expect him to encourage the church by telling of the better days ahead, but he says the opposite. He declares that the worst is yet to be. "Fear none of those things which thou shalt suffer: behold, the devil shall cast some of you into prison, ... and ye shall have tribulation ten days." Of course ten days here is not to be taken literally. It only means that they are to be tried for a brief and definite period. During that period there is to be imprisonment, ending for some in martyrdom. Some of them were headed out toward ghastly death. It was, therefore, to a slandered, poverty-stricken, and persecuted church that was facing yet greater persecution that the Master said, "Thou art rich."

III

What, then, were its assets? What did the membership of this church possess that made it rich in spite of its liabilities?

A. The members of this church were rich in the possession of a Saviour who could enter into full sympathy with them. "I know the blasphemy and persecution and poverty." That means far more than that their Lord simply knew their situation. It means that he knew through his own experience. He knew because he had been tempted in all points just as they were being tempted. If they were being slandered, he understood since he had been slandered. If they were being persecuted, he had passed through that experience before them. If they were poor, he had been more destitute than the birds, more homeless than the foxes of the mountains.

What a privilege it is, when some great tragedy falls upon us, to know the comfort of an understanding friend! The other day a mother in my city lost a little child. A neighbor came in to comfort her. She talked beautifully. But the brokenhearted mother listened without seemingly receiving much comfort. When she had gone, another mother came who did not talk half so well; but she had a little high chair at home in which nobody sat any more, a few toys with which nobody played. She put her arms around her friend and simply said, "There, there, I understand." And that understanding had healing in it. But how much more healing there is in the understanding of One who is "able to do exceeding abundantly above all that we ask or think."

B. These saints were rich in convictions that they felt were worth living for, and, if need be, dying for. "Be thou faithful unto death," is the Master's appeal. "Faithful" here means convinced. It is to be convinced of the faithfulness of Christ himself. That is an attribute of God with which the saints of the Old and New Testaments are constantly steadying themselves. They were sure that God would never fail them, that he would never let them down. Their confidence in his faithfulness enabled them to be faithful. Because they were sure of their Lord, they could stand up and take it in an evil day while others without their faith went to pieces.

While visiting in Scotland, I was interested in that great rock against which Fitz-James is said to have leaned his back as he met his foes with these brave words:

> Come one, come all! this rock shall fly
> From its firm base as soon as I.

These Saints of Smyrna were in a hard situation. They were few among many. But they refused to play the coward. They refused to give over the fight. They leaned their backs against the solid conviction of the faithfulness of God and were steadfast. "I have set the Lord always before me: because he is at my right hand, I shall not be moved."

Not only did their convictions enable them to stand up and take the worst that their foes could inflict, but they kept them loyal even when they could not understand. They refused to let Christ down even when it looked as if he had let them down. That is magnificent.

I remember a story that, when I was a boy, used to move me to tears. It told of an Englishman who long ago went on horseback to a certain village to collect a sum of money. As he was returning with his gold tied to his saddle, he stopped at the roadside at noon to eat his lunch. With him was his faithful dog who was his constant companion. He untied the sack of gold and set it beside him that it might not be out of his reach at any time. After he had eaten, he fell asleep for a few moments. Then he mounted his horse and continued his journey. But he forgot his gold. The dog began to run in front of the horse and bark and turn back, but the man went on his way. Then the dog began frantically to snap at the horse's heels and turn back. But still his master did not understand. At last he decided that his dog had gone mad. With great reluctance he turned in his saddle and shot the dog through the head. The faithful beast looked at him with questioning eyes; then he dropped in his tracks, and the man went on his way. But he had not gone far until he discovered his loss. Then he understood. At once he put his horse to a run and hurried back. He came to the place where the dog had fallen. The road had a crimson stain, but the dog was gone. When he reached the gold, there was his dog with a paw on either side and with his chin resting upon the treasure. He was dead. He had not understood, but he had remained loyal unto death.

These people were steading themselves by solid convictions and were holding to their loyalty even when God seemed to have forgotten them.

C. Then these saints were rich in the possession of a good will that all the slander and persecution of their enemies could not destroy. When they were hated, they refused to give way to hating. When they were lied about, they did not deal in lies. They did not declare that they would get even with their enemies at any cost. Had they done so, they would have become like their enemies. Jesus could hate sin without hating the sinner. We have a great tendency, as someone has pointed out, to hate the sinner and to love his sin.

One day a brilliant young man was preaching in Jerusalem. He so antagonized his audience that they dragged him outside the city and mobbed him. They stoned him to death as we might stone a snake by the roadside. Though he was so heavily outnumbered, I can imagine Stephen might have successfully hurled a stone or two and thus have gone down fighting. But he did not. Instead he went down praying, "Lord, lay not this sin to their charge." Thus he died with a light in his face that even death could not blow out. "They saw his face as it had been the face of an angel." When the ugly scene was over, it certainly looked like miserable defeat for Stephen, but in reality it was everlasting victory. There was at least one man present who could never forget. That was a young man named Saul. The shining face of Stephen haunted him. He could not resist a man who could throw about the shoulders of his murderers "the sheltering folds of a protecting prayer." I am quite sure that the fact that a little later this great soul was saying, "Lord, what wilt thou have me to do?" was due, under God, to Stephen more than to any other single influence.

These saints at Smyrna had convictions that gave them courage to stand in the face of danger. They also had a Christlike good will which the worst that their foes could do could not change to hate. That is something that the world cannot imitate. It was the one characteristic of Christ that has perhaps won the heart of men above all else. When bold Simon thought of that in his Master that moved him supremely, I think it was this: "When he was reviled, [he] reviled not again." It is this good will that goes on loving that wins all the victories that are permanent. Force may triumph, but its triumphs are always temporary. These saints, therefore, were to be congratulated because in the face of bitter persecution they maintained a good will that was akin to that of their Lord.

D. Finally, the members of this church were rich in the possession of a quality of life over which neither persecution nor poverty nor death could have any destructive power. Though pillaged and peeled, they were not utterly impoverished. In fact, their sufferings had only made them the richer. Their want brought them greater wealth. Their weakness was a pathway to power. Their crucifixion was enabling them to be crowned. They were learning through their own experiences what Paul had learned through his. "We know that all things work together for good to them that love God."

This they were finding to work in the here and now. They were sure it would still work beyond this world with its griefs and graves. When, therefore, the Master said to them, "Be thou faithful unto death, and I will give thee a crown of life," they knew that he was not speaking of any material crown. He was not offering them some fading laurel wreath. He was offering them life at its best in the here and now. These saints had found a life that was good today. They were sure that it would be good tomorrow. They were sure it would be good when they were passing through the Valley of the Shadow. They were sure it would be good when they had passed "to where beyond these voices there is peace."

"Thou art rich." I wonder if our Lord can say that to us as a congregation. I wonder if he can say it to us as individuals. What treasure do you possess in the here and now that is worth living for and worth dying for? What have you that will abide? What have you that neither failing banks nor wrecking worlds can wrench out of your hands? If you have no wealth that is real, then the fault is your own, for the riches possessed by this church are for every one of us. "Though he was rich, yet for your sakes he became poor, that ye through his poverty might be rich." If we were to claim all that he is offering us this morning, it would make us the envy of the angels.

3
The Unfinished Sermon

And as Paul reasoned of righteousness, temperance, and judgment to come, Felix trembled, and answered, Go thy way for this time; when I have a convenient season, I will call for thee (Acts 24:25).

I

Felix was a black sheep. He was so very black that he was conspicuous, even in a day when this color was more prevalent among politicians than it is today. Born a slave, Felix had managed in some way to win his freedom. Not only so, but by dint of considerable ability and of far more rascality he had worked his way up to a position of power. But in spite of his lofty position, he was still a moral pigmy. Whatever sovereignty he had was on the outside of him. Within, he was still in bondage. Tacitus tells us that he ruled in the spirit of a slave with all cruelty and lust. He was, therefore, the very last man that we expected to find looking toward the heights in seeming quest of a better life.

But even this hardened man had one big moment that was full of promise. As this scene opens, we are greeted by a joyous surprise. We find Felix at church. This does not mean that he has gone out to God's house, but that he has brought God's messenger to himself. He has sent for Paul to hear him concerning his faith in Christ. Sad to say, Felix is at this service with a heavy handicap. Beside him is a woman who is not his wife. She is the wife of another. This woman is a Jewess by the name of Drusilla. She has had a better opportunity religiously than Felix, but she has made little of it. She is as fair outwardly as she is rotten inwardly, which means that she is a very beautiful woman. But in spite of this sordid relationship, in spite of his soiled past and his dirty present, Felix has come to church. He has done so of his own free will. That in itself gives us hope.

Why, I wonder, did this renegade attend this service? What has brought him to church?

A. He may have been prompted by mere curiosity. He knew something of Paul. He had met him face to face. Only yesterday he had presided at a brief court session where Paul was at once the prisoner at the bar and the attorney for the defense. The preacher had handled his case with such consummate skill as to win the grudging admiration of Felix. There was no mistaking the fact that this prisoner was no ordinary man. Even his enemies had to confess that he had turned the world upside down. Perhaps Felix wanted to see his amazing prisoner at closer range. Therefore, he sent for him and sat under his ministry, but with no higher motive than idle curiosity.

B. Felix may have sent for Paul because he was bored. When Felix had won his freedom, he chose a name for himself that signifies "happy." But Mr. Happy was not in reality happy at all. He was tired, bored, fed up. Though he had given reign to every lust, life had lost its tang. Felix was greatly in need of a new thrill. There is pleasure in sin, of course, but it soon grows stale. This is because sin has nothing new up its sleeve. It has been well said that if a rake from Babylon were to come back and visit our night life, he would stifle a yawn and say, "I saw all this in Babylon more than twenty-five centuries ago." Maybe Felix attended this service because he was bored.

C. Felix may have been present because of a desire for material gain. Luke tells us that, when later on, he sent for Paul, it was in the hope that Paul would give him a bribe for setting him free. If Felix was thus trying to capitalize on his church attendance, he would not be in a class entirely by himself. There have been those thoughout the centuries who have sought to use the church. Some have made it a smoke screen behind which to hide their rascality. Others have attended because they had something to sell, or were eager to advance their ambitions. I am quite certain that there are comparatively few of these. Yet, there are some, and Felix may have been of this number. He may have listened to Paul with no higher motives than those that prompt a gambler to take part in a game of chance.

D. But suppose we give this royal rascal the benefit of the doubt. Suppose we assume that he attended this service because he really had a hungry heart. Suppose that we concede that there was still growing in the fetid soil of his soul, like a white flower, a longing for a better life. This is not an unreasonable assumption. Such longings have stirred, times without number, in the hearts of men just as hopeless and hard as was Felix. What faithful minister has not spoken with fear and trembling to some man regarded as hopeless, to find himself answered, not by insults as he feared, but by eager longing and penitential tears? It may be, therefore, that Felix was at church, even as you and I, because he was possessed of an insatiable hunger for God.

But after all, while the motives of Felix in attending this service are of importance, they are not of supreme importance. The proprietor of a certain department store has this motto pasted behind the counter, where it can be seen only by his salesmen: "It is not what the customer comes in after, but what he goes out with, that matters." So it is with church attendance. Many that have come to scoff have remained to pray. This is Paul's hope as he faces Felix.

II

What did Paul have to say to this sinner and his paramour? Suppose we slip in and share the pew of Felix and Drusilla. Do not let the suggestion shock you. They are sinners, I know, but so are we. The difference between us is one of degree rather than of kind. Therefore, what Paul said to them he is saying to you and me. Let us then, along with them, take our place at the feet of this messenger of God.

It is a favorite comment that Paul in his message to these desperate sinners has nothing to say about the love of God. One commentator remarks that we have heard of the love of God till some of us have grown love-sick. But it is my conviction that Paul's sermon is motivated and shot through with love. Love is the very warp and woof of it. I am sure of this because of the effect it had upon the hearer. It is true that love is not mentioned in the fragment of the sermon that we have, but bear in mind that Paul did not get to finish his sermon. The physician had hardly finished diagnosing the disease before the patient walked out on him. Felix adjourned the meeting. He left the service before the benediction. Therefore we have only a part of Paul's sermon, that part that was meant to search this man's soul. Look at it!

A. Paul reasoned of righteousness. I like that word "reasoned." He did not rant. He did not merely beat the air. He did not go off in sentimental gush. He reasoned. He spoke of the sanity, the thoroughgoing common sense, of being right and of doing right. He showed that sin is insanity. In doing so he was taking his cue from his Master. Jesus once told the story of a graceless laddie that left a home of love and plenty to starve in a hog pen. He explained the boy's conduct, not by saying that he was too clear-headed to stay at home. He said rather that he was beside himself. The stupidity, the madness, of the wrongdoer is seen in the fact that such a one flings himself against the forces of the universe. The very stars in their courses fight against him.

The one supremely sane something, on the other hand, is righteousness. A righteous God can give his full sanction to a righteous man, and to none other. He can put all his infinite resources at his disposal. Righteousness, therefore, is fundamental. There is no really sane living without it. Surely there is no vital Christianity without it. No amount of work, no amount of religiosity, nothing, is a substitute for right living.

When the early apostles were arrested and commanded to leave off their preaching, they gave this heroic answer, "Whether it be right in the sight of God to hearken unto you more than unto God, judge ye." What is the meaning of this answer? This is what they are saying: "Our first purpose is not to save our own skins. It is not to win applause. It is not to have an easy time. Our one purpose is to do the right as God gives us to see the right." That is to be our one purpose. Absolutely nothing can take the place of that. The call of this hour and of every hour is for righteousness, rightness. We need to be right with God and right with man. We need to be right in all our relationships, national and international. We need rightness between capital and labor, rightness in public office, rightness in the home. We need to handle the tools of our daily trade as religiously as we pray. Naturally, therefore, Paul reasoned of righteousness.

B. Paul reasoned of temperance—self-mastery, self-control. He spoke of temperance to a man who was dressing his soul in chains. He spoke of self-control to one who had put the reins of his life into the foul hands of his lusts. He spoke of self-mastery to one whose passions and appetites were bullying him and scourging him and bringing him to heel like a common cur. He tried to make Felix see something of the tragedy of changing a habitation meant for the Holy Spirit into a pigsty. He tried to bring him to the realization that self-reverence, self-knowledge, self-control, these three alone, lead to sovereign power. He spoke home to this man's need. He reasoned of temperance.

C. Paul reasoned of judgment to come. Ministers of yesterday used to preach quite a bit about judgment. But it has been a long time, I dare say, since you heard a sermon on this subject. Yet the Bible speaks of judgment again and again. And there is always sanity in what it says. I find it easy to believe in a judgment to come because of the judgments of the past and of the present. Judgment is something that is taking place all of the time. God is constantly coming in judgment upon nations and upon individuals. Where are the bloody despotisms that once flourished upon the banks of the Euphrates and the Tigris? Where is mighty Rome with her far-flung tyrannies? God came in judgment upon them and said, "Depart ye cursed," and they passed away. Where is the Europe that went mad in its lust for power before the World War? God came in judgment upon it, and it slipped into an abysm of blood and tears. What of the Europe that was made by a treaty born of hate and revenge? That Europe is experiencing the judgment of God at this moment, and is therefore hanging upon the verge of the abyss.

As God judges the world, even so he judges the individual. This he does in the very nature of things. Every time I stand at the forks of the road and take the lower instead of the higher, I undergo judgment. This is my sentence: I find it easier, ever after, to take the lower road and harder to take the higher. When I face the light and refuse to see it, I am judged in that I lose, in some measure, my capacity to see. When I hear the truth and refuse to respond to it, my sentence is that I become a little more dull of hearing. When my heart is stirred by the wooing of the

Spirit and I refuse to yield, my sentence is that I lose my sensitiveness. Paul reasoned of righteousness, of temperance, and of judgment.

III

What effect did this sermon have on Felix? Here is the way I should have expected this story to read:

"As Paul reasoned of righteousness and temperance and judgment to come, Felix sneered. Felix laughed outright in gleeful scorn. 'You are trying to frighten me,' he chuckled. 'Don't you know that I have run past such childish rubbish long ago? Don't you realize that I am smart enough to know that all your commandments were made by men to frighten timid souls into being good? Don't make me laugh!'" But this was not his reaction.

No more did Felix get angry. When Paul began to talk about being right to a man who knew he was wrong, when he spoke of self-mastery to one whose lusts had him bridled and saddled, the preacher was getting fairly personal. In the language of the farm, "he was plowing close to the corn." It would have been very natural for this royal sinner to have resented such plain preaching. He might easily have glared at the Apostle and said, "You are my prisoner. You can't talk to me like that. Such bold words are likely to cause you to land in a dungeon." But renegade that he was, he did not get angry.

What then, I repeat, was the effect of Paul's sermon? "As Paul reasoned of righteousness, temperance, and judgment to come, Felix trembled." How amazing! As I watched him, I saw him clinch his fists till his knuckles grew white, and his nails bit into the palms of his hands. I saw the big beads of perspiration break out on his face. I saw him shake like a man in the grip of a heavy chill. Then with a cry that was half a sob he shouted, "It's enough, Paul. I know you are right. I know that it is reasonable that a man should be right. I know I ought to be master of myself instead of the slave of myself. I know it is reasonable to expect judgment. You are right. But I have heard enough. Go thy way for this time. It is not convenient for me to respond to your message today. When I have a moment," as Moffatt translates it, "I will call for you."

Thus Felix interrupted the Apostle just as he was reaching the climax of his sermon. Had he waited a moment Paul would have told him of a Christ that was able to make him right at the center of his being. He would have told him that, just as leperous Naaman's flesh came back to him like the flesh of a little child, so he could be made anew. Had he only listened a little longer, Paul would have told him of One that could set him free, in whose fellowship he need never come into judgment. But the sermon was never finished. Felix adjourned the meeting and left, in the truest possible sense, without the benediction. In later days he sent for Paul again and again. But he never trembled any more. For two whole years he lived in the same house with this great saint, but that privilege was worth no more to Felix than if Paul had been a mummy. Felix had missed that high tide of the Spirit, that, taken at the flood, would have led him to life eternal.

IV

Why did Felix fail? Why did he face his big moment only to throw it away?

He did not fail because of ignorance. He could not blame his failure on the fact that he did not understand Paul. He could not claim that the whole business was too deep for one like himself who had no head for religion. He understood far too clearly for his comfort. Therefore, he could no more plead ignorance than you and I. We confess that ours is a day of moral confusion. Many of us have so lost our skyline that we cannot tell where the earth leaves off and the heavens begin. At times we are glad to lay blame for our wrong choices on this confusion. But the truth is the other way around. It is not so much that our moral confusion has led to wrong choices as that our wrong choices have led to moral confusion. Our trouble, as that of Felix, is not that we know too little; it is rather that we fail to live up to what we actually know.

No more did Felix fail because his clay soul was so shattered as to be beyond remaking. That is never the case. He failed because he refused to give God a chance. God, through his prophet, woke him up; but that was all that even God could do. He wakes us, but we must do the getting up ourselves. When I was a schoolboy I used to get up by an alarm clock. There were times, however, when my clock called and I failed to respond. The result was that I remained in bed. The further result was that the next morning it failed to wake me. Felix might have risen into newness of life, if he had only responded to Paul's appeal.

But, though deeply moved, Felix was not willing to pay the price. There was a woman at his side more hardened in the ways of sin even than himself. So far as we know, she was not moved in the least. In fact, I can well imagine that she looked upon both blazing preacher and trembling hearer with superior scorn. Felix dared not defy that scorn. Then there was a yet greater difficulty. For Felix to respond would mean that he must give up Drusilla altogether. That he could not do. At least, not yet. Thus when he might have been free, he remained a slave.

His is an oft-told story. Felix belongs to that vast company that come very near to doing something worthwhile and yet fall short. They are the almost folk whose stories are unspeakably pathetic. We meet them in every walk of life. Bret Harte tells of such a man. This man went to California during the gold craze of 1849. He staked a claim and began to dig. Day after day he toiled, but in vain. At last he stuck his pick in the earth, turned away in disgust, and sold his claim for a song. But the purchaser had hardly turned the dirt into which the pick had been stuck before he found signs of gold. Soon he was the proud possessor of one of the richest veins in all that famous field. He became a millionaire. Meantime the man who had first worked the claim was making his way back home with pockets as empty as the pockets of a shroud. In the after days he doubtless thought how very near he came to being rich, but he was a pauper just the same. Felix came near to being rich spiritually, but he remained a moral bankrupt.

Some fail, as did Felix, because they never come to the point. They feel the spell of Jesus, but never dare to rise up and follow him. Years ago I walked away from a service with a schoolmate. The tides of the Spirit had run high in that service, and my friend had been greatly moved. "I came very near going forward tonight," he said to me with desperate earnestness. Again, as we came to where our roads parted, he said wistfully, "I came very close to dedicating my life to God tonight." But he failed. By and by a destroying habit laid hold on him, squeezed the fine juices from his life, and flung him away. But I can never forget that he almost became a Christian.

There are others who fail because, though they decide, they do so halfheartedly, or for some reason fail to follow through. These dwell in the suburbs of Christianity, never venturing down into the heart of the city where the lights are bright and where the great traffic of the soul is carried on. They are religious, but their religion is of a kind that satisfies neither God nor man. This is the case because almost to do a thing is not to do it at all. Almost to find life is only to find death. Therefore, I am calling my own heart, as well as yours, to a full dedication to Him who is able to do for us and through us beyond our power to ask or think.

4
Mother Ostrich
(Mother's Day)

The daughter of my people is become cruel like the ostriches in the wilderness (Lam. 4:3).

My text, you see, is from Lamentations. It is quite at home in the book of which it is a part. It is a lament. It staggers under a weight of grief. Every word is baptized with tears. But this text is more than a lament. It is a sharp and cutting rebuke. It is full of hot indignation. The prophet wields it in honest anger, as if it were a scourge. The terrible wrongs that are being perpetrated before his eyes, while breaking his heart, arouse his soul to battle. He cannot look on without a protest.

I

Who is it that has thus stirred the prophet's grief and indignation?

Strange to say, it is not some worthless father. In those distant days, the father had quite an assured place in the family. Of course he has lost it with the passing of the years. Today he is the family joke. Here is a story that is typical: Little Johnnie had a dearly loved dog named Laddie. One day, while Johnnie was at school, Laddie got in the way of a passing car and paid the penalty. Johnnie's mother was distressed. She hardly dared tell her son of his sad loss. She thought once of telling him that the dog had strayed off. But she made up her mind that the truth must be told. So, when he came in from school, she said quite timidly: "Johnnie, Laddie was killed today." To her surprise he said, "He was?" and then went on upstairs to his play. Now, it so happened that Nurse was upstairs. She undertook to give Johnnie some details of the tragedy. At once there was a loud wail, and Johnnie came hurrying downstairs, sobbing as if his heart would break. Naturally his mother was puzzled. "Why," she asked, "are you weeping so over what Nurse said when you did not seem to mind at all when I told you that Laddie was dead?" As Johnnie struggled with his sobs, he answered, "I thought you said 'Daddy.'"

But here is a rebuke directed not against the fathers of that day, but against the mothers. Surely this prophet was quite a daring man! It takes all the courage that I can muster even to repeat his words. For this is Mother's Day. It is the day that we have set apart to honor her whose love is about the most beautiful and enriching something that this world knows. To this end we have come together, wearing red carnations for the living, and white carnations for the dead. We feel deliciously sentimental. Tears are waiting just out of sight, to rush eagerly upon the scene as soon as they receive their cue. Naturally, in an atmosphere like this, these rude words of the prophet seem strikingly out of place. They jar and disappoint us. They arouse our antagonism, and leave upon our tongues a tang of the downright sacrilegious.

Now, with your resentment I have no slightest quarrel. In fact, it does you honor. It is an indication of your love and loyalty to your own mother; to her whose living presence is now perhaps your dearest joy; or whose home-going has left you your most precious memories. We all agree, I am sure, that there is no crown too resplendent to be placed upon the brow of motherhood at its best. But this prophet is daring to remind us of what we are very prone to forget on an occasion like this, and that is that motherhood in itself is not of necessity a badge of either goodness or greatness. A thoughtless, flippant, and self-centered woman is not necessarily transformed into a saint the moment she becomes a mother. There are those who remain vain, and selfish, and heartless to the end of the chapter. There are those who live and die without any realization that, in becoming mothers, one of the deepest and sweetest secrets of human blessedness has whispered itself to them, without ever being heard. It is against this type of mother that the prophet brought his bitter accusation.

II

What is the charge that he made against the mothers of that far-off day? He did not charge them with unfaithfulness to their marriage vows. He did not charge them with being mere giddy, gossiping gadabouts. He did not accuse them of spending one half of their time at the beauty parlor and the movies and the other half at the card table. He did not accuse them of blowing cigarette smoke into the tender eyes of their babies, or of keeping them awake at night by the loud hilarity of cocktail parties. He brought against them an accusation big enough to include all these, and more. He charged them with the ugly crime of cruelty. "The daughter of my people is become cruel like the ostriches of the wilderness." Cruelty, at its best, is indifference to suffering and pain. At its worst, it is a positive delight in these.

Now, we realize at once that the crime here charged is one that is exceedingly ugly. Cruelty has never been beautiful, but it is a sin against which we of today are peculiarly hostile, especially in its cruder forms. We hate it, perhaps more than any generation that the world has ever seen. There are a good many vices that we view with indifference. There are quite a few that we have learned at once to endure, to fondle, and embrace; but cruelty is not one of them. Thanks to the Gospel of the tender Christ, the human heart has grown more sensitive with the passing of the years, till today the sight of crass cruelty makes almost all of us to burn with indignation.

For instance, in our city a few weeks ago, some men were being pestered by a mangy dog that haunted their filling station. The dog was masterless and homeless, with nobody to take his part. Therefore, partly to be rid of him, and partly out of sheer cruelty, these men dashed a bit of gasoline on him and struck a match to him. But, in spite of the fact that the dog had no master, the perpetrators of this cruel deed did not escape. The people of the community were so aroused that they had them arrested; and if I am not mistaken, they spent a few days in jail. If they did not, they deserved to do so, for they were needlessly cruel. Now, it is with the crime of cruelty that these mothers are charged, a cruelty infinitely worse than that of these thoughtless men. They are accused of being cruel to their own children.

III

What is the nature of their cruelty?

It is not the aggressive type. These mothers were not accused of inflicting any positive wrong upon their children. They were not thrusting them into some dark coal pit to do a man's work with their undeveloped bodies. They were not inflicting on them any physical harm. Had you accused them of doing so, they would have doubtless told you that they had never laid the weight of their hands upon one of their children. Their children knew nothing of kicks and cuffs. There are very few maimed bodies today because of aggressively cruel mothers. That has always been the case. These mothers of the long ago would no more have thought of inflicting positive bodily harm upon their children than the mothers of today.

What form, then, did this cruelty take? It was a cruelty, the Prophet tells, like that practiced by the ostrich. The writers of the Bible do not think highly of this bird. She is, to them, a symbol of cruelty and forgetfulness. Job describes her in this graphic fashion: "She leaveth her eggs in the earth, and warmeth them in the dust, and forgetteth that the foot may crush them, or that the wild beast may break them. She is hardened against her young ones, as though they were not hers." That is, the cruelty of the mother that so enrages the prophet is the cruelty of neglect. She cannot be bothered. She is too busy having a good time, has too many social engagements, belongs to too many clubs, to be worried by such small matters as her own children. Sometimes she is so absorbed in saving the world that she has no time for the saving of her own home.

Once, such a mother was my next-door neighbor. She never missed an opportunity to lecture on the importance of the right training of children, but she left her own largely to the nurture of the street. A cartoon of a few years ago draws her picture. A forlorn rooster is standing beside a hen's nest. The nest is full of eggs that are just beginning to hatch. Some of the chicks are half out of the shell. But the hen is nowhere in sight. A friend passes and asks the rooster as to the whereabouts of his wife. As the big tears run down his face, he answers: "She's down at the Mother's Club giving a lecture on 'How to Hatch Eggs!'" This type is with us still, but thank God, she is in the minority.

IV

Why were these mothers so cruelly neglecting their children? Their neglect, I am sure, was not born of ill will. Not a mother among them ever set out deliberately to make her child a menace to himself and a menace to society. Nor was their cruelty born of utter indifference. It is a rare mother indeed who does not yearn for the best for her child. What, then, lies back of this neglect? There were doubtless a number of reasons. I am going to mention only three:

A. These mothers failed to recognize the fact that the child is of supreme value. They were, therefore, taking the fine gold of childhood, the Prophet charges, and treating it as if it were but commonplace earthenware. A recent historian has charged the downfall of Rome to the failure of her mothers. There was a time when that mother who displayed her sons as her jewels was typical of the best mothers of the empire. Those were the days of her greatness. But when they lost their sense of the supreme value of the child, then came her days of darkness and downfall. This prophet was wise enough to know that the nation that fails to give the child first place is headed for disaster. Therefore he rebukes in words hot and passionate.

But it ought to be far harder for us to fail to set a proper valuation upon the child than for those of that far-off day. Since then Jesus has come. He is the supreme champion of the child. When his disciples asked him, "Who is greatest in the kingdom?" he did not point to any king or philosopher. He took a little child and set him in the midst. So important is the child, he tells us, that the angels that are of highest rank are the ones that have the care of children. "In heaven there angels do always behold the face of my Father." So important is the child that he solemnly warns against despising or undervaluing this treasure. "Take heed that you despise not one of these little ones." So important are they that he walls them in with a grim wall of millstones saying, "Whoso shall offend one of these little ones, it were better for him that a millstone were hanged about his neck, and that he were drowned in the depth of the sea."

But why is the child so vastly important? Of course it is important as the maker of tomorrow. Soon everything that we possess is going to slip from our nerveless fingers into the hands of our children. That is worthy of consideration. But that is not the sole secret of the child's vast importance. A child is not important because of its physical strength; it has little. It is not important because it is a money-maker. In this respect it is a liability rather than an asset. A child is supreme, not simply because it is the highest and most intelligent of animals. Jesus put the child first because he recognized the supreme worth of the spiritual. And only as we share his convictions are we likely to join him in giving our boys and girls their place of supreme importance.

B. These mothers may have neglected their children because they failed to realize the terrible tragedy that is born of neglect. This is also true, I am sure, of a great many mothers today. Of course we recognize the deadlines of neglect in the realm of the physical. If there is a little baby in your home, you know that all you have to do to bring about the death of that baby is simply to let it alone. Neglect of its physical needs spells disaster. That we readily recognize. Not long ago a mother was executed in Germany. Her crime was this: She received a dole from the government for the support of herself and her children. But she was a pleasure-loving woman and squandered it all upon herself. The faces of her children became more and more pinched. At last they died of starvation, and this mother was arrested, tried for murder, and executed. And we feel that the sentence was just.

But our children have other hungers than those of the physical. They hunger for the Bread of Life, and thirst for the Water of Life. "The tongue of the nursing child cleaveth to the roof of his mouth for thirst," cries the indignant prophet. He knows that even children have hungers that cannot be banished by bacon and beans. Everybody ought to have wisdom enough to see that. In 1930, three thousand carefully selected leaders in child welfare met at the White House Conference for the study of the child. After the findings had been discussed, they summarized them into a Children's Charter covering nineteen points. The first was this: "For every child spiritual and moral training to help him to stand firm under the pressure of life." But that spiritual and moral training is just what is being sadly neglected today in countless homes. There are those even in the Church who, through their neglect, are rearing their children in practical paganism.

Now, the tragic cost of this cannot be estimated. I have in mind now a father and mother who are typical of all-too-many modern parents. They themselves were reared by parents who were more or less active in the Church. In their youth they attended, at least spasmodically. But now they never attend any more. Their children have never attended either Sunday school or church. On Sunday they go to the movies. They are as utterly devoid of any religious training as if their father and mother were both confirmed atheists. Yet they are the product of a so-called Christian home. And these are by no means exceptions. No wonder there is a widespread moral breakdown. Children cannot get along without religion any more than adults. A certain judge said the other day that of the more than four thousands boys under twenty-one that he had sentenced, only three of them were attendants on Sunday school. How much longer will it take for us to realize the fact that our Dillingers and Clyde Barrows are not so much born as made; made by mothers and fathers guilty of the cruel sin of neglect?

C. The final reason I mention for neglect on the part of these mothers was their failure to realize the rich rewards of the mother who is willing to pay the price that real motherhood involves. There are many fine and rewarding tasks at which a mother may work, but by far the most rewarding of all is the training of her children. What are some of the rewards of the mother who, in the fear and love of God, earnestly performs this high and sacred duty?

1. She has the reward that comes from having to give without stint, and that is the living of a full, rich life. It is costly to be a mother. "There stood by the cross of Jesus, Mary, his mother." The place of motherhood at its best is always beside the cross. Hers is a daily dying to self. But for that we should not pity her. For it is this daily dying that is the open roadway to the life abundant. If you have tears to shed, keep them for

the thoughtless mother who lives for herself. The woman of all others to be envied is she who, through her daily giving, compels those who know her best to rise up and call her blessed.

2. The second reward of the mother who is faithful to her task is that of giving to the world strong and useful sons and daughters. Here is a mother in a hard situation. She is a slave. But one day she holds a baby to her heart that is so beautiful that, though death sentence has been pronounced against him, she simply cannot let go. "By faith Moses, when he was born, was hidden three months of his parents because they saw that he was a proper child; and they were not afraid of the king's commandment." They take a basket and line it with pitch and prayer and hide the little fellow among the rushes of the Nile. By and by in the providence of God he is back in his mother's arms again. She faithfully trains him during the few short years that he is hers. Then one day we read of him this fine word: "By faith Moses, when he was come to years, refused to be called the son of Pharaoh's daughter, choosing rather to suffer affliction with the people of God than to enjoy the pleasures of sin for a season." That was his own faith, but he had learned it at his mother's knee.

> She shot the deathless passion in her eyes
> Through him, and made him hers, and laid her mind
> On Him, and he believed in her belief.

It is to mothers such as this that humanity owes its greatest debt. It is to such that we, under God, look with hope for tomorrow.

5
A Father's Failure
(Father's Day)

O my son Absalom, my son, my son Absalom! would God I had died for thee, O Absalom, my son, my son! (2 Sam. 18:33).

Here is an exceedingly bitter cry. It tends to make our blood run cold after all these years. There are tears upon it that have not been dried by the hot suns of the centuries. Who is this that is giving way to such an abandon of grief? Surely it must be some woman, some mother perchance, whose empty arms are aching for the laddie that she has loved and lost. No, that is not the case. This is not the wail of a woman, but of a man; not of a mother, but of a father. It is King David breaking his heart over what he regards as the greatest failure of his life.

I

Wherein has David failed? Surely his failure is not full-orbed. In many respects he has been vastly successful. The story of his thrilling career reads like a romance. He has come up from the ranks. Once he was only a shepherd lad with no great standing even in his own family. But he had a mind that was as brilliant as the kiss of sunlight upon clear water. He was possessed of a dauntless courage. If tradition is correct, he had a genius of a poet. While, at his worst, he was a great sinner; at his best, he was a great saint. Then he was vastly attractive. Upon all with whom he came into contact he cast a spell that was all but irresistible. Then, too, he was a practical man of affairs with his feet firmly fixed on the ground. He was a many-sided man, eminently fitted by nature to make good in any situation.

And make good he did. He climbed by rapid strides till he became king, not by right of birth, but by right of ability. As king he served his people well. He proved himself at once a great soldier and a great statesman. He soon succeeded in welding a few scattered, quarreling tribes into a compactly organized nation. He made a success financially. Much of the vast wealth that went into the building of the Temple came through his hands. In fact so wisely did he reign, that his people, throughout their subsequent history, looked back to his day as the Golden Age of Israel. Had he lived in our day we should doubtless have written a book about him entitled "From Shepherd's Tent to King's Palace." This book would certainly have found a place in "The Success Series" and have become a best seller.

In what, then, did this greatly successful man fail? He failed as a father. As a result of that failure, the body of his handsome, gifted, and favorite son is now lying, a crushed wreck in a pit in the wilderness. Therefore, while others would surely have been thrilled by the reading of David's biography, I seriously doubt if he himself could have read it with any real satisfaction. The very brilliancy of his success in certain directions must have served to give only the greater emphasis to his failure in another. As he read he would have realized that his winnings had been many and worthful. He had certainly won a secure place in the hearts of his people. But in spite of all this, the book would have left him cold. He would have been made to feel that, after all, he had majored on minors, and that his success, though very real, had been bought at too great a price.

And this is the record of so many men who are otherwise successful. I have in mind a certain gentleman who out of small beginnings succeeded in building a fortune of several millions. His brilliant success as a financier blazoned his name to the world and made him at once an object of envy and of honor. But his wealth, I am told by one who knew him well, became a weight instead of wings. It caught and held him somewhat as a piece of flypaper catches and holds a fly. In his efforts to be free, he was at times little better than a madman. Of course he had little or no time for his family. His boys grew into soft and pulpy manhood. They were far less suited to cope with their situation than their hard-working father had been to cope with his. When he died, his gold seemed to sweep over them a bit like an avalanche. They were completely swamped by their unearned wealth. Thus this father, while proving himself a conspicuous success in the building of a fortune, proved himself a yet more conspicuous failure in the building of men.

A few years ago, at one of our state fairs, a crowd was gathered about a prize hog. That hog was about all that a hog ought to be. His hair was parted in the middle and nicely combed. His hoofs were manicured in such a fashion as to have roused the envy of a movie star. Everybody who saw that hog realized that the man who raised him knew his business. Now, the boy who was set to look after this hog seemed to have been chosen as a foil to further emphasize his perfection. He was a little wizen-faced, hollow-chested, hatchet-heeled fellow who seemed bent upon burning up all the cigarettes in the world, and that as quickly as possible. He would not have walked a mile, I dare say, for his favorite brand, for he did not seem to have strength enough. He had too evidently found his unlucky strike. But the most startling fact about the whole situation was this: The father of the boy and the owner of the hog was the same man. In the hog business this father was a huge success. In the boy business he was an utter failure. And in spite of his vast abilities this also was one of the tragedies of the life of David.

II

But why does David take his failure so hard? Why is his heart so completely broken?

A. It is broken because of his deep and tender love for the son that he has lost. This I say, in spite of the fact that he was only a father. Fathers are not generally credited with doing much loving, you know. They are not supposed greatly to care. To be convinced that this is the common view, it is only necessary to contrast the celebration of Mother's Day with that of Father's Day. On the former we come together in greater numbers. We come with our largest handkerchiefs, for the atmosphere is redolent of sentiment, and we are ready at the slightest provocation to burst into tears. On Father's Day we still bring our handkerchiefs, but we use them to stifle our yawns rather than to dry our tears. However unlike the Master dad may be in other respects, he is at least like him in this, that he has made himself of no reputation.

Now, this lack of popularity is, of course, in part, his own fault, but it is not altogether so. In my opinion it is at once unfortunate and unfair. I believe, as another has suggested, that a golden halo for mother is altogether fitting. It blesses both us who give and her that receives. But I believe also that it would be good, if we could find in our hearts to do so, to give a "little tin halo" to father now and then. It might serve to encourage him to do better. Then I ask it in the name of fair play. As I think of my own mother I think of one who was sunny and full of laughter, with never a thought of herself. As I think of my father, I think of one who was more rugged and stern, but whose unselfish devotion to his own could no more be doubted than hers. David is a father, but in spite of the fact his heart is broken over the loss of his boy.

B. Then David is crushed because his loss is without remedy. There are some mistakes that we can correct. Having blundered, we may promise ourselves to do better next time. But in many instances there is no next time. That is the tragic note in that "exceeding bitter cry" of Esau. We read that afterwards when he would have inherited the blessing, he found no place for repentance. That does not mean that God refused to forgive him. It only means that he found no way of undoing the past. He could not get back into yesterday and have placed in his hands again the big opportunities that were his on life's bright morning long ago. What was done could never be undone. It is this realization that makes the grief of David all the more bitter. He is facing the fact that of the things that have no next time, one, at least, is the rearing of a son. How many things he now feels that he could do for Absalom were he only a little boy again! But that can never be. Therefore, there is the agony of utter hopelessness in his cry, "O my son Absalom, O my son, my son Absalom! would God I had died for thee!"

C. But the note of supreme bitterness in the sorrow of David, that which brings his grief to its tragic climax, is the haunting fear that the boy that he has lost hopelessly he has also lost needlessly. He has lost him when he might have saved him.

"Had I only been a better father to him, had I only acted differently," he keeps telling his tortured soul, "then he would be with me now instead of yonder in the pit, under the stones. I have lost him and it's all my fault." This is the nagging fear that becomes a conviction that he cannot shake off. It is a conviction that bites like a serpent and stings like an adder. His loss would have been hard enough if he could have persuaded himself that he had done his best. But this he cannot do. His hell is that such a persuasion is impossible.

One day in Texas a farmer was in the field plowing cotton. With him were his two small boys. He looked up from his task to see a large dog coming toward them. This dog was snapping at the cotton stalks, and the farmer saw that he was mad. At once he put himself between his boys and the dog. He told them to run for refuge to a nearby cotton bin, while he kept the dog away. The boys made good their escape. But not so the father. He was forced to fight the dog, and that with no weapon but his pocket knife. As a result he was bitten from his face to his feet. Medical science could do nothing for him. But during his lucid intervals, as death crept upon him, he would look into the face of his wife with a smile and say, "Don't you worry about me. I saved our boys." And he went out to meet God unafraid. I think he could have done so, even if the boys had died with him, seeing that he did his best. But to lose when we might have done better, that is "sorrow's crown of sorrow." And that is the pathetic plight of David. He has lost his son—lost him hopelessly, and lost him needlessly.

III

How did David come to make this terrible failure?

He did not do so, I am sure, because Absalom was born a traitor. He was born with a capacity for treachery, but he was also born with a capacity for faithfulness and loyalty. "What manner of child shall this be?" was asked by a group who stood about the cradle of John the Baptist. Is there any sure answer to such a question? The Catholic Church has always believed that there is. As it looks into the face of a little child, it says without hesitation, "This child will be a Catholic." The Jews believe that there is an answer to that question. As they look into the face of a baby, they do not hesitate to say, "This child will be a Jew." But Protestantism is often far less sure. That is one of our chief weaknesses. Too often we answer, "The Lord only knows!" And then hurry about our business or pleasure. Yet both the Scriptures and experience teach that if we train a child in the way he shall go, when he is old, he will not depart from it.

If, then, David did not fail because failure was inevitable, why, I repeat, did he fail? There are, I think, two outstanding reasons.

A. He failed because he shifted the responsibility for the care of his son upon the shoulders of others instead of taking it upon himself. What he did in this last scene is, I think, typical of his entire relationship to Absalom. When his soldiers were going out to battle, a battle that was to determine whether he himself was to keep his crown and his life, it was not of these that he was thinking. He was thinking only of his loved and treacherous son. "Deal gently for my sake," he told his officers in the presence of the army. "Deal gently, for my sake, with the young man, Absalom." But when the army had marched out of sight, he was doubtless very uneasy. "My officers are good and loyal men," he probably kept telling himself. "Still I am greatly afraid for my son. I should have gone myself. Yes, at all costs I should have made the safety of my boy a personal matter."

But who is that coming across the plain? It is a messenger. The king is all solicitude, but his anxiety is only for his son. "Victory!" the messenger shouts through panting lips. But the father has no ear for such a message. There is but one question, "Is the young man Absalom safe?" The first messenger did not have the heart to tell, but yonder comes another, "Victory!" he shouts also. But David asks that same eager, anxious question, "Is the young man Absalom safe?" Then comes the tragic answer, and David is a broken old man. "O my son Absalom," he sobs, "I am so sorry now that I did not go out even at the cost of my life. Better a million times that I should be lying under the stones than you."

Now, what David did in this instance, I repeat, he has done through the years. It is true that he has a good excuse for his conduct. We are in no sense disposed to judge him harshly. He has been a man of many cares. He has been burdened by matters of state. Naturally he has not had much time for his children. But we cannot shut our eyes to the pathos of it all. For, as a result, he never really got acquainted with Absalom, never gained his confidence, never won his heart. In his younger years, when he had a broken toy, Absalom never thought of going to his father about it. Nor did he think of doing so in later years when he had a broken heart. Father and son were both most fascinating, but they never became friends. And yet David gave Absalom everything except himself. But failing to give himself, he failed altogether. Thus he lost a treasure far more priceless than his crown.

How David would have envied the humble father of whom his son could say this:

> He's the best thing, daddy is,
> When he ain't got the rheumatiz,
> Gives me pennies and good advice,
> 'Bout keeping clean and being nice,
> Saying please, and don't deceive,
> Handkerchief, instead of sleeve.
> Seems just like 'at daddy knew,
> He was once a small boy, too.
> Second table for him, I spec,
> With nothing but the chicken neck.
> Anyhow he always says,
> Give the kid the best there is.
> And when Ma sends me off to bed,
> He always takes the light ahead,
> And holds my hand and talks maybe,
> About the things that used to be,
> When he and Uncle was little boys,
> And all about their games and toys,
> What am I gonner be, Gee whiz,
> I'm gonner be like daddy is.
> I'd rather be like him, 'ijing,
> Than president or anything.
> He's like Ma says angels is
> When he ain't got the rheumatiz.

But David was too busy. As so many today, he "passed the buck," lost his boy, and broke his own heart.

B. The second reason for David's failure was his bad example. There was a time, after he had become a father, that he allowed himself a most tragic visit to the far country. He became a prodigal. In utter disregard to his obligations to others, he took a woman to whom he had no right. Later he murdered her husband to conceal his crime. No wonder that when his oldest son wanted a woman for himself, he took her ruthlessly, even though she was his half sister. Had not his father set him the example? And that father, having done so, dared not punish his brutal son. Thus Absalom felt called upon to take vengeance into his own hands and punish his brother. All this brought an ever-widening chasm between himself and his father until it ended in utter tragedy. No wonder, therefore, that David felt, and rightly so, that he had the blood of his ruined boy on his own hands. He had employed two most effective methods of destruction, a bad example and neglect.

But, you answer, was not David a good man? Yes, David repented of his terrible sin and God in his mercy forgave him. But, while David's repentance brought him personal salvation, it did not bring salvation to his wayward boy. David made one excursion into the far country, and Absalom followed his steps; but when David came back, so far as this son was concerned, he came back alone. That is a tragedy that has happened times without number. Years ago I had a neighbor who was the father of a large family. He was a drinking man, though not a drunkard. He was friendly toward religion, though he seldom went to church. But when he was between fifty and sixty years of age, he was soundly and happily converted. How hard he tried to atone for his wasted years! How eager he was to reach his children, all of whom had now grown to manhood and womanhood! I have seen him stand up in the little village church to read a bit, only to burst into tears. But his children were not softened by these tears—they were only shamed by them. They went with him into the far country, but the poor broken father came back alone. May God save us from such a tragedy! That he may do so, let us as parents in the fear of God take the responsibility for the welfare of our children upon ourselves.

6
The Work of the Evangelist

Do the work of an evangelist (2 Tim. 4:5).

I

"Evangelism" is a beautiful word that has lost its winsomeness. Somehow on its journey from the Jerusalem of yesterday to the Jericho of today it has fallen among thieves that have wounded it and stripped it, and departed, leaving it half dead. It takes a rather rash Samaritan, therefore, to dare turn aside to set this poor chap upon his beast and take him to an inn and take care of him. This is especially true because a veritable procession of priests and Levites are passing by, not only refusing to lend a hand, but, we fear, inwardly chuckling at the plight of the poor fellow, and secretly hoping that they are soon to see the last of him.

Now, this has not always been the case. I am not among the ancients, but I can remember when the first day of the revival brought the people together in unusual numbers and with heightened expectancy. And I have seen multitudes come together greatly wondering, saying, "What do these things mean?" because there were big events taking place that could only be accounted for in terms of God. But that is largely of yesterday. The announcement of a revival in the average church is no longer a clarion call for the rallying of the hosts of Zion. It is rather a warning gong that calls, "To your tents. O Israel." Our people, even some of the best, flee for refuge to the security of their homes, or to their cars on the open road. The announcement of a revival today in the average city church would be about as effective in bringing together a congregation as if the pastor were to say, "My brethren, next Sunday we are to have on exhibition in this church some very interesting cases of contagious disease. If you come and bring your families, you may be able to contract one or more of them."

As to just how this change has come about, it is not my purpose fully to explain. Of course, I know the one on whose shoulders we are accustomed to lay the heaviest part of the responsibility. It is upon the professional evangelist. But, of course, no fair-minded man would make a wholesale condemnation of these ministers. Some of them are the salt of the earth. They are holy men, the latches of whose shoes I personally feel myself unworthy to unloose. But there was a type of which this was not the case. You remember how they used to come with their high-powered methods and their veteran sermons that had done yeoman service in many a hard-fought campaign, but had not grown shorter, but rather longer. For you know an old sermon is a bit like a snowball rolling down a hill—it grows larger all the time, but what it accumulates is generally rubbish. These brethren often had a genius for counting sham results and real money. They reigned as kings for a few days, and then folded their tents like the Arabs and silently went away, leaving us on four flat tires spiritually, and with our spares stolen.

But even for this type of spurious evangelism the evangelist was by no means solely to blame. An equal, if not a heavier, part of the responsibility must be put upon the pastor and his people. Often when we invited the evangelist we did not do so because we were eager for a real refreshing from the presence of the Lord. We were rather seeking a smooth road out of a hard situation. We wanted a million-dollar return on a five-cent investment. We were eager for a bumper crop without giving ourselves to the prosaic task of clearing and breaking and tilling the soil. This counterfeit evangelism, I am sure, has done much to bring the genuine into disrepute.

Then there are those who look askance at evangelism because they feel that it has been too individualistic and has demanded too small a sovereignty over life. But, in my opinion, our lost passion for evangelism is due more to our lost sense of

God than to any other cause. "Then said I, Here am I; send me" is the testimony of one who years ago burned with a hot enthusiasm for sharing the blessings that had come into his own life. "Then"—this is a backward-looking word. Upon what does it look? It looks back to the time when Isaiah had seen "the Lord high and lifted up"; to the time when in the light of that vision he had seen himself as a sinner, and had been made clean. The fires of evangelism always burn in hearts that are conscious of the Divine Presence. And when men lose that consciousness, the fires go out.

II

Just what do we mean by evangelism? Its simplest meaning, as you know, is to tell Good News. But to understand it fully we need more than a definition—we need to see it in terms of personality. Let us, therefore, turn to the Supreme Evangelist. Mark, in his romantic and aggressive Gospel, shows him to us with peculiar clearness: "And Jesus came into Galilee preaching the Good News about God." He told men that they were all the sons of God, that it was every man's privilege to call God "Father." He showed how life's supreme tragedy consists in our effort to be independent toward our Father. That was the tragedy of the graceless laddie of whom we read in the fifteenth chapter of St. Luke. He went away from home, not because he wanted to grieve his father, but because he wanted to be independent of him. But life was transfigured for him the moment he determined to take a son's place in his father's house.

By telling men that they are all the sons of God, he told them the further Good News that they were brothers one to the other. He told them that no man need live as a stranger in this world, that men need no longer glare at each other across frozen chasms of indifference, or fiery chasms of hate—that every man might see in his fellow a brother. And Jesus not only preached brotherhood, but he lived it. He put himself under every man's load. He dined with outcasts. He talked to harlots with the same gracious courtesy that he showed to the purest of the pure. Thus he dug a chasm between himself and decent folks and went to the cross for doing the work of an evangelist.

But after Jesus had been crucified, men who had been baptized into his spirit took up his message. One gifted young man, by the name of Stephen, evangelized so compellingly in Jerusalem that "they were not able to resist the spirit and the wisdom by which he spake." Unable to answer him with words, they mobbed him. But though they stoned the life from his body, they could not stone the radiance from his face: "They saw his face as if it had been the face of an angel." Though they robbed him of his life, they could not rob him of his love. He died with this Christlike prayer upon his lips: "Lord, lay not this sin to their charge."

Among those having a part in this ghastly crime was a young man who was about the best intellect of his day. He tried to forget the ugly memory by giving himself to an orgy of persecution. But he was never able to brush the beauty of that radiant face from his mind. He was never able to stop his ears to that Christlike prayer. At last, on the way from Jerusalem to Damascus, Paul surrendered and fell upon his face, and cried, "Lord, what wilt thou have me do?" He then rose to his feet to do the work of an evangelist. He, along with certain nameless nobodies, went about over the Roman Empire establishing little "colonies of heaven."

These colonies were made up of men and women who did not fear the world's fears. They were men and women who were not gripped by the world's greeds. They were not divided by the chasms that divided others. The pagan world looked on with wistful wonder and exclaimed, "How these Christians love each other!" And because they wanted to love and be loved, they were drawn into these little groups. Thus the Lord added unto them day by day such as were being saved. And as they increased in numbers, they increased in power. Out from them flowed rivers of living water that had a perfectly amazing capacity for withering all that was selfish and unclean, and for making all that was beautiful to grow. The Roman Empire took knowledge and tried to destroy them. But the more they were killed, the more they lived. At last they became so mighty that they displaced the Roman eagle with the cross. Then they began to fear the world's fears, and to be gripped by the world's greeds. Then the sun went down and the night came on, the night of the Dark Ages that lasted almost a thousand years.

Then centuries went by, and England is in the throes of a terrible reaction from Puritanism. And Christianity seems to many a dead and exploded theory. But one night there came out of a little service in Aldergate Street a man who declared that he had felt his heart strangely warmed. That man mounted his horse the next day and set out on an evangelistic tour that carried him literally through the century. And out of his hot heart there breathed upon England a veritable Gulf Stream. At the kiss of its warmth the icicles fell from the eaves of the houses, the winterstripped trees put on their verdant foliage, the flowers bloomed, the birds sang, and the heart stood up in the glad consciousness that God had come. Every reader of history knows today that by far the biggest event of that eventful century was the evangelism of John Wesley and his followers.

III

And now we come to our bewildered and perplexed day. It is a day of cynicism, a day of disillusionment, a day of bitter hunger of heart. Some poet a century from now might sing of large areas of the life of our day:

> On that hard pagan world, disgust and secret loathing fell,
> Deep weariness and sated lust made human life a hell.

Multitudes are "between two worlds, the one dead, the other powerless to be born." But our desperate need is at once our challenge and our opportunity. Surely multitudes both within the church and out of it are realizing as never before that there is none other name under heaven given among men whereby we must be saved but the name of Jesus.

The call of the hour, therefore, is for the right kind of evangelism. It is only as we evangelize that we shall build up the body of Christ. Doing the work of an evangelist builds up the evangelist himself. There are multitudes even in our churches to whom Jesus Christ is as vague and dim as the shadow of a dream. Is there a roadway to spiritual certainty? I am sure that there is. Jesus is still coming to seek and to save that which is lost. If you and I set out on the same quest, our roads and his are sure to run together sooner or later. We will come face to face with the Christ who is doing what we are undertaking to do. For if any man is willing to do his will, he shall know. We shall also build by capturing from without. It has been my habit through the years to give an opportunity at every service for men and women to make a public confession to Christ. Many times I have called when nobody has responded, but the vast majority of calls have not been in vain.

While seeking the lost, we are to realize that our most fruitful work is not with adults, but with childhood and youth. It is still hard for some to believe this. A fine old gentleman said to me after a service that I had had with the boys and girls, "I do not believe in services of that kind." "Why?" I asked. "Because," he said, "Ten or twenty years from now some of those boys and girls could not tell you when they were converted." "What of it?" I asked. "Why," he said, with vehemence, "I would not give the pop of my finger for any man's religion who could not tell you the day and the hour in which he was converted." Now, if you know when you were converted, thank God for it, but remember this: there may be one sitting beside you who is more beautifully conscious of the Divine Presence than you are, who does not know.

When I was a boy, my father gave me a little colt. He gave me that colt the very day it was born. I began at once to get on good terms with it. I would rub its nose and stroke its ears. Now and then I would give it an apple core (if I could spare it). Then at last I dared to mount that colt and go for a ride. Never once did he throw me, or kick me, or paw me. If you had asked that colt three years later, "When were you converted into a work horse?" he would doubtless have answered you in the language of Socrates, "Search me."

But there was another colt about the same age as mine, to which nobody paid any particular attention. One day my father said that he was old enough to be converted into a work horse. Therefore we chased him out of a pasture into the lot, and out of the lot into a stable. We bridled and harnessed him and plowed him beside a maturer horse. Then we unhitched him and let him out to where the ground was soft. We called a friend in whom we had a personal interest and asked him if he would be so kind as to mount. And when he mounted, the back of that colt went up like the apex of an isosceles triangle, and the brother erased himself. Finally, after he had thrown a few more men, after he had torn up one or two pairs of harness and kicked the spatter board out of the buggy, a strong man could drive him provided he was tired. If you had asked him three years later when he was converted, he would have said, "I shall never forget it as long as I live. It was a a terrible ordeal." But I submit to you that my colt was broken in a far more normal and a far more natural way. All of which leads me to say that the best field of evangelism is the home, for the only sure way to have Christians is to raise them.

Finally, if we are to do the work of an evangelist, we must be willing to pay the price. Evangelism is costly. There is no twilight sleep process for the bringing of newborn souls into the kingdom. It is only as Zion travaileth that she brings forth sons and daughters. That is the reason that an ease-loving church like ours shies away from it. We do not like to be bothered. The passionate words of the saints sound to us a bit like a foreign tongue: "And now, behold, I go bound in the spirit unto Jerusalem, not knowing the things that shall befall me there; save that the Holy Ghost witnesseth in every city saying that bonds and afflictions abide me. But none of these things move me." And here is rugged John Knox crying, "Give me Scotland or I die." We rather say, "Give me a comfortable bit of Scotland, or I will move." Too few of us believe in evangelism enough to be eager to pay the price. But where the price is paid, results are sure.

Several years ago I was conducting a revival in a little town where there were seven or eight churches that had just enough interest to quarrel among themselves. The meeting was going badly, and I was desperately discouraged. At last I tried to have a testimony meeting, and the testimonies dwindled into discouraging and critical sermonettes. Just as I was preparing to close the service in despair, a gentleman stood up that I came to know intimately, and to honor and love with genuine devotion. His presence was not prepossessing. He was rather shabbily dressed. He used bad grammar. But what redeemed him from commonplaceness was a marvelously illuminated face. It looked like it had a sunrise behind it, and you felt yourself almost unconsciously peeking round to see where the light came from. He turned that wonderful face toward me and said, "Brother, I thank God that things are just as they are." I looked at him in wide-eyed amazement. But he went on to explain: "I love to get in a hard place for my Lord. I love to get in a place that is so hard that there is no chance to get into without you get down on both hands and knees and crawl through to God." I saw that he knew a secret with which I was too little familiar. After this testimony, we dismissed and went home.

In the evening service that followed, the tabernacle was crowded to overflowing. There was a mourners' bench that ran entirely across the tabernacle. It was long enough to have accommodated at least a hundred mourners, though one an inch long would have been long enough for what we had been having. I stepped out on this mourners' bench and began my sermon. I had been preaching only two or three minutes when this brother came and kneeled down beside me, and as he prayed I tried to preach. And, account for it how you may, the atmosphere was utterly changed. I saw strong men come from out the dark to kneel at the altar, but before they could get on their knees they rose into newness of life. "And the place was shaken where we were assembled together, and we were all filled with the Holy Spirit." And it is my conviction that the church will never rediscover the lost secret of its evangelistic power till it learns again the high art of prayer. Let us therefore take to heart the challenging words of our text, "Do the work of an evangelist."

7
Poverty that Makes Rich

Blessed are the poor in spirit: for theirs is the kingdom of heaven (Matt. 5:3).

What an audience this is that faces the Master! The inner circle is made up of his special friends. Beyond them stretch acres of human faces. It is a vast throng. It is made up of all kinds and conditions of men. It is a cross-section of humanity. There are the successful and the failures. There are those who have conquered and those who have been defeated. There are the rich and the poor. There are the literate and the illiterate. They are, doubtless, of varied races and varied religious creeds. In fact, as Jesus speaks to this multitude he is speaking to a miniature world.

But as he looks into their faces, as he looks beyond their faces into their hearts, he sees that they are all out on the same quest. They are all seeking for the same thing. Most of them are seeking blunderingly. They have been disappointed and are doomed to further and deeper disappointment. The pathos of their blind gropings lays hold on the Master's heart. It suggests to him a theme for the sermon of the hour. "Every heart here," he says to himself, "is in search of happiness. But they have missed the way, most of them. I can do nothing better than point out the way that they have missed." Therefore he said: "Blessed are the poor in spirit: for theirs is the kingdom of heaven."

The audience that Jesus faced in that long ago is very close akin to the audience he would face were he to come to our city this morning. The heart of humanity remains unchanged through the years. Were he to stand in Court Square today and speak, he would still be moved with compassion as he looked upon the multitude. He would still see them scattered and harassed as sheep without a shepherd. He would still find folks doing a thousand different things in order to be truly happy. He would only find a few who had laid hold on the open secret that is so often hid from the wise and prudent and revealed unto babes. He would take little account of our scientific discoveries and inventions. He would tell us that the roadway to happiness is the same today that it was nineteen centuries ago. He would have no better direction to give than that given in our text.

And Jesus can speak with authority about happiness, because it was his constant possession. I am not forgetting that he was a man of sorrows and acquainted with grief. But in spite of that his was the gladdest heart that ever beat in a human bosom. His was the sunniest face that ever looked out on this world. And those who share his poverty of spirit share his happiness. Sorrow may come, but it will only be temporary. "Joy cometh with the morning." It is happiness that abides. It is sorrow and sighing that flee away.

I

Who are the blessed folks? Who are those that find real happiness?

Jesus makes it plain at once that our happiness is not born of any outward conditions or circumstances. This is a truth that lies right on the surface. It is one that has been established by the experiences of countless millions, yet it seems that every man has to learn it for himself. We still have a feeling that the happy man is the one who achieves outward success. Blessed is the man who makes a fortune. Blessed is he who can write a check in seven figures. Happy is the man who has a palace in the city and a summer palace by the sea or in the mountains. Blessed is the man that has won the applause of his fellows. Blessed is the woman who has become the darling of society. But Jesus says that happiness is not born of what we have.

No more is it born of what we fail to have. When Luke reports this sermon he says: "Blessed are the poor." But poverty is not in itself a blessing. Since it tends to give one a sense of need, it may more readily become a roadway to real happiness than riches. Riches tend to give a false independence. But no man is necessarily blessed simply because he is poor. Nor is any man necessarily unblessed because he is rich. Dives blundered out into the dark. Lazarus found a place in Abraham's bosom. But Dives was not condemned because he was rich, any more than Lazarus was saved because he was poor. One may be just as poor as Lazarus and yet be greedy and grasping and wretched, while another may be as rich as Dives and yet be truly blessed.

When I was a boy there was a rather notorious character in our community who pretended to farm. In reality, however, with the coming of spring the song of Buffalo River cast its spell upon him, and he went fishing practically every day. Now and then, on Saturday afternoons, some farmer who had caught up with his work would go fishing and get Uncle Zeke's fishing place. This gentleman would return from his noon meal to find himself crowded out. Then he would say piously: "You can stay here and fish if you like; I have a family to support." With that he would turn on his heels, go out to the little village, borrow a chew of tobacco, and sit in front of the store and talk theology. And this is what he would say: "Well, I'd rather be a poor man and go to heaven than be a rich man and go to hell." But nobody ever believed that Uncle Zeke was absolutely sure of entrance into the pearly gates simply because he was miserably poor.

Happiness depends not upon what we have, nor upon what we do, but upon what we are. If we seek happiness on the outside, we shall miss it forever. Happiness, if it ever comes, must come from within. It does not depend upon the kind of house in which we live; it depends upon the kind of man that lives in the house. It does not depend upon the kind of garments in which we dress; it depends upon the kind of individual that is dressed. The kind of man that is happy, said Jesus, is the man that is poor in spirit. He arrives, and he alone.

How utterly ridiculous this must have sounded to some who were listening! How absurd was such a declaration to that Roman, for instance, whose nation had its foot on the neck of the world! How absurd it must have sounded to the Jews who were even more proud than the Roman! It still sounds unbelievable enough even to us. There were those that heard it that day who glanced at each other knowingly, shrugged their shoulders, and swaggered off down the mountain side saying that the Preacher was mad and that there was nothing of real worth in what he was saying. We try to be a little more respectful, yet there are millions to-day who are just as far from believing this statement as the audience to which it was first spoken.

"Blessed are the poor in spirit." "Maybe so," you reply, "yet I cannot work up any enthusiasm for such poverty." But even if you are only half convinced that the poor in spirit are blessed, of one thing you may be sure—that the proud in spirit are unblessed. Here is a truth that not many will deny: Wretched are the proud in spirit. Did you ever see one afflicted with proud flesh? Proud flesh is about the most sensitive something that I know. There is only one thing that is more sensitive and that is a proud spirit. You may be proud of your pride, but of this you may be sure—it is a certain road to wretchedness. Miserable are the proud in spirit. Happy are the poor in spirit.

II

But what does Jesus mean by poverty of spirit? Maybe our lack of enthusiasm for this treasure grows out of our misunderstanding. To be poor in spirit does not mean self-contempt. Jesus never tells us to despise ourselves. He never asks any man to crawl and cringe and grovel. He discovered to us the worth of the individual. He believed that the meanest human soul had immeasurable possibilities, might realize a glorious destiny. To be poor in spirit, therefore, is not to despise yourself. It is not to look upon yourself with contempt. It is to be humble, childlike, teachable, ready to lean upon a higher power.

In order to really understand poverty of spirit it is necessary to see it become incarnate in a personality; otherwise it tends to remain a mere abstraction. The same is true even of so familiar a something as love. I asked a group of little folks sometime ago, "What is love?" and they were utterly silent. I then asked: "Did you ever see any love?" At once every hand went up. They could not define love according to the International Dictionary. Even if they could have done so they would have been little the wiser. But they knew love, nonetheless. They had seen love become human life. This they had done as they had looked into mother's face and had felt the kiss of mother's lips and experienced the tender ministry of mother's hands.

Where, then, shall we look for poverty of spirit? Maybe the ten spies will serve as an illustration. They went into Canaan to spy out the land. They came back with a sense of their utter littleness and worthlessness. They declared whimperingly: "We saw the giants that live over there, and we were in our own eyes as grasshoppers. There is no use to undertake to go forward with the enterprise. We can never succeed. God has done nothing more than play a grim joke on us. The whole enterprise is no more than madness." But these men were not poor in spirit; they were poor spirited, and nothing more.

Then we might try the man with one talent. One day he came from his master's presence with a treasure in his hand. That treasure indicated that he was trusted. It showed that his master had confidence in him. He gripped it proudly and thought of the many high adventures that he was going to have with it on the marts of trade. But as he was going to make his first venture he met a friend who had two talents. That dampened his ardor somewhat. Then he met another who had five. After that his zest and ardor went ice cold. He said: "This one little talent is nothing in comparison with what these others have. I will stand no chance at all." So he crept away back home, slunk out into the garden as the shadows gathered, and hid his talent in the earth. But he was not poor in spirit; he was full of pride and fuller still of cowardice.

Where, then, shall we go? Answer: to Jesus himself. These beatitudes are descriptions of the character of our Lord. It is to him, therefore, that we go to find one who in the deepest and fullest sense was poor in spirit. He was so poor in spirit that he said: "I can of mine own self do nothing." He was so poor in spirit that he one day girt himself with a towel and washed the feet of a little handful of men, fishermen and taxgatherers and such like. What a menial task! It was far too mean for any of the disciples. Had I been host that day I might have said to Peter: "Simon, the servants are all out. There is no one here to wash the feet of my guests. You are the leader among them. Suppose you do it." Simon was an excellent man, but he would have bristled and said: "Are you talking to me? You think I am going to wash the feet of Judas and Thomas, of James and John? They are always arguing with me that they are going to be greater than I in the kingdom. If their feet don't get washed till I do it, they will go unwashed forever. Are you trying to insult me?" "No," I might have answered, "I am trying to crown you."

But what none other would do Jesus did. Why? Because he had no respect for himself? No, that was not the reason. Look at the state of his mind as he did this. "Knowing that he was come from God and went to God." That is, when he was conscious of his divine origin, when he was conscious that he was going to sit down at the right hand of his Father to receive a name that is above every name, then he girt himself with the towel. Here is true poverty of spirit. Here also is manhood at its best.

III

Why is it that poverty of spirit leads to happiness?

A. It is through poverty of spirit that we come into possession of the kingdom of God. Not that the kingdom is given to us as reward. There is nothing arbitrary about it. "Blessed are the poor in spirit: for theirs is the kingdom of heaven." Such enter naturally, and the door is closed to all others. One day when the disciples were having one of their oft-recurring disputes as to who should be greatest they brought the matter to Jesus. In answer to their question Jesus took a little child and set him in the midst of them and said that the most childlike should be the greatest. Not only so, but that without childlikeness, which is none other than humility or poverty of spirit, it is impossible to enter the kingdom at all. "Except ye be converted, and become as little children, ye shall not enter into the kingdom of heaven."

Jesus told a story of two brothers. The older brother was a steady, hard-working chap who seemed altogether dependable. He kept constantly at home and gave himself with diligence to his duties. But his brother was a waster. He ran away and squandered the wealth his father had given him in riotous living. But though this elder son remained at home and worked, there was never a feast given in his honor. He himself said he had never had so much as a kid with which to make merry with his friends. But one day, as he was returning from the field, he was greeted by the sound of music. He came a little nearer, and the whole household was astir with wildest revelry and joy. Naturally he was concerned to know what was going on. Therefore he called a servant and asked what it meant, and the servant said: "Your brother has come home, and your father has killed for him the fatted calf."

Little wonder that this steady worker was a bit indignant at the turn things had taken! Why did the father show such seeming partiality? It was not that he cared nothing for hard work, but rather set a premium on dissipation. The difference in the treatment of these two sons grew out of what they were in themselves. The elder son reveals himself thoroughly. "Lo, these many years do I serve thee, neither transgressed I at any time thy commandment." That is, he insists that he had never sinned; he had always been perfectly upright. He was, therefore, in no sense poor in spirit. The younger son, on the other hand, had nothing better to say for himself than, "I have sinned against heaven, and before thee, and am no more worthy to be called thy son." The doors of the feast opened before him automatically, because he was poor in spirit.

B. Then, it is only through poverty of spirit that we remain in the kingdom. Pride certainly goes before destruction, and a haughty spirit before a fall. There is a deal of truth in that classic story of the frog that decided to seek a warmer climate. At first he could think of no fit conveyance in which to go. At last he hit upon this happy contrivance. There were two wild geese that were friends of his. He found a string and asked each one of the geese to take an end. As they did so, he seized the string in the middle. These geese rose into the air, and the frog found himself hurrying toward the land of his dreams. But a spectator from far below, looking up, saw the strange sight and shouted: "Who invented that?" The frog's pride would not allow him to keep silent. He shouted back: "I invented that." But in so doing he let go of the string, and his questioner a moment later was looking upon a bit of minced frog. As in the case of a vast multitude, his pride had been his ruin.

Jesus had a friend who was devoted to him. But this friend was at times a bit proud in spirit. Jesus saw that this was going to undo him, so he undertook to warn him. "All ye shall be offended because of me this night." And Peter took it as personal and denied it flatly. He said: "I cannot speak for these others, James and John and Andrew and the rest. They may fail you, but you can certainly count on me. Though I should die with thee, yet will I not deny thee." And Peter went out in the strength of this confidence to utterly fail. No wonder when he had wept his way back to God he urged his friends to clothe themselves with humility as with a garment. "God resisteth the proud, but gives grace to the humble."

C. Then, poverty of spirit leads to blessedness because it fits us to serve in the kingdom. When the wise man names the six things that God hates, one of them is a proud look. In that we are exactly like him. No one offends us more deeply than the individual who undertakes to lord it over us. It is the man who identifies himself with us, the man of poverty of spirit whose ministry we welcome and find helpful. "Brethren, if a man be overtaken in a fault, ye who are spiritual restore such an one in the spirit of meekness." It is the only way we can restore them. If we go in the spirit of pride, in the spirit of self-sufficiency, we shall repel rather than restore.

F. B. Meyer tells this story: On one occasion he was stopping at a hotel in Norway where there was a little girl who was very fond of playing the piano. But she played only one tune, and played this with just one finger. Naturally she became a bit of a nuisance. When the guests were awakened by her each morning, they would endure it as long as possible, then make their escape as best they could. Now, it so happened that one of the greatest pianists of Norway came that way. He was awakened the next morning along with other guests by this tuneless pecking on the piano. He hurriedly dressed and went down into the parlor that the little girl had all to herself. He made himself acquainted with her, told her that he knew the song that she was playing, and asked that he might play it with her. She consented, for she was poor in spirit. He, therefore, took her upon his lap and drowned her discord with his own marvelous melody. And so it may be for ourselves. If in true humility we give first place to the Supreme Master, he will surely touch our heart harp and change its blundering discord into the exquisite music of abiding blessedness.

8
The Peacemakers

Blessed are the peacemakers: for they shall be called the children of God (Matt. 5:9).

"Blessed are the peacemakers." For nineteen centuries this great word has been knocking at the shut doors of men's hearts, largely in vain. We have said "Yes" with our lips, but by our lives we have said: "Blessed are the sowers of discord. Blessed are the fomenters of strife. Blessed are the war makers." But Christ in loving patience still proclaims that it is the peacemakers who are blessed.

I

Now, to make peace is to do far more than merely abolish strife. To make peace is to do more than cause men or nations to be peaceable. We may keep the peace without having peace. We may bring about a cessation of strife without in any real sense being peacemakers. The Roman Empire brought about peace within her borders, but she was not a peacemaker according to the meaning of Jesus. Her subjects had not lost the will to fight. They kept peace through fear. They were not at war solely because the dread of Rome forced them to swallow their hate and to submit with sullen rage to their fortune.

When I was a boy we owned two magnificent dogs. These dogs were of different breed. They had a natural antipathy to each other. Now and then, they would come to open war. When they did so they fought to utter exhaustion. Having reached this state, they would cease to tear at each other, but they would still glare at each other in such a fashion as to indicate that the only reason they were not fighting was because they could not. And that was the impression that one received as he traveled among the nations of Europe just after the World War. One could not but feel that the only reason they were not at each other's throats was because they had already fought to complete exhaustion. They had been bled white. Therefore the peace that existed was a peace born, not of good will, but of weakness. It was a purely negative peace.

Then, there may be peace that is the outcome of mere indifference. Rip Van Winkle and his wife were accustomed to have some very stormy sessions in their humble little home. But by and by these domestic wars ceased. The noise of conflict was no longer heard. How had this peace come about? It had not come because husband and wife had arrived at a better understanding. It had not come because they had agreed, out of mutual love, to be more forbearing. There was peace because one day Rip took his musket upon his shoulder and strolled off into the mountains for a twenty-year nap. I read some months ago where two deadly enemies met and shot each other to death. As they lay side by side they were at peace, but it was the peace of indifference, it was the peace of death. Therefore it was a purely negative something.

But the peacemaker of whom Jesus speaks does a positive work. He puts an end to strife by the bringing in of its opposite. He does not pull up the noxious weeds of discord and enmity and hate one by one and leave the garden bare. He rather sows and cultivates such a luxuriant crop of the flowers of the Spirit—love, joy, peace, long-suffering—that the disturbing weeds are all crowded out. He drives out suspicion by confidence, enmity and misunderstanding by understanding and good will. He puts brotherliness in the place of unbrotherliness. He puts love in the place of hate. Through his ministry men not only cease to fear each other and to fight each other, but they come to love and to trust each other. He does more than take the sword and break it into fragments. He does more than blunt the spear and burn its shaft. He beats the sword into a plowshare, and the spear into a pruning hook. He converts the implements of war and waste into implements of peace and prosperity. He overcomes evil with good.

II

Now, that peacemakers are needed in our world no one will deny. The peacemaker is a benefactor. I take it that he is the supreme benefactor.

A. We need peacemakers because there is such a widespread lack of peace. Strife and discord, hate and misunderstanding are on every hand. This I say not minimizing the marvelous advancements that have been made. No man can look upon our world with open eyes and fail to recognize that there has been encouraging progress. The fact that the Prime Minister of England has recently crossed the Atlantic to talk with our President in the interest of world peace is surely the prophecy of a better day. But there still remains much land to be possessed. In spite of all that has been done, our peace is not yet like a river. We are still far from a "parliament of man and a federation of the world."

Think, first, of the strife between man and his Maker. This strife is as old as human history. In the Eden story, man after his sin no sooner heard the voice of God walking in the garden than he hid himself. He had come to fear the One that he should have loved best. Instead of seeking God, instead of crying in his need, "O my God, where art Thou?" God had to do the seeking and cry, "Adam, where art thou?" This is an old story, I know. You may no longer believe it. But surely you believe the more modern story of your own life. Account for it how you may, some of you are keenly conscious of the fact that there is a quarrel between you and God. There are many, thank God, for whom this quarrel has been healed. But there are vast multitudes for whom it has not been healed. The supreme tragedy of their hour is that there are so many in our world that are not on friendly terms with God.

With the loss of peace between man and God there comes also the loss of peace between man and his better self. That has always been the case. To be at war with God is to have civil war within your own soul. "There is no peace, saith my God, to the wicked." If I could take my soul into my own two hands and utterly erase the image of God from it, I might have a certain kind of peace apart from God. But this I cannot do. It has been well said that no man can be as bad as he wants to be. The hogs may be content within the pigsty of the far country. But for the prodigal, contentment is impossible. He was made for something better. He is persistently tormented by memories of his father. He is made miserable and restless by dreams of his finer possibilities.

"My soul cleaveth unto the dust" is the cry of the Psalmist. Then why does he not lay hold on the dust and be content? Because he cannot. The cleaving is all very real, but that is only half the story. "My soul cleaveth unto the dust; quicken thou me according to thy word." That is the other half. While he cleaves to the dust, he also aspires to the heights. While with one hand he fingers the mud, with the other he reaches after the stars. Why does not the sea lie down within its far-flung shores and be at rest? Because the heights will not let it alone. When it is minded to become content with the earth, the voices of cloudland call it. Therefore it is always tossing and restless. And man is forever like that troubled sea till he finds rest in God.

Then there is widespread discord and strife between man and man. Men glare at each other individually. Group looks askance at group. Racial prejudices and racial hates abound. Nation glares at nation, and each proclaims itself *the people*. Many Americans still say, "America first"; Many British, "England first;" Germans, "Germany first." We are still far from seeing in every man a brother for whom Christ died. We are still far from a brotherhood of nations.

B. Then we need peacemakers because strife and enmity and hate are so costly. It is certainly true that the most expensive something in all the world is hate. Think of its cost to the individual. Enmity between God and man is the fountain source of all wretchedness. It was when Paul looked to the heights and went toward the depths that he cried, "O wretched man that I am!" Such hostility makes for ineffectiveness. This it does because it makes for a divided personality. "Unite my heart to fear thy name" is the wisest of prayers. It is the only way that we can come to the fullness of our powers. A divided personality means at once the loss of happiness and the loss of our highest effectiveness. A unified personality, on the other hand, means the attainment of both peace and power.

How costly is hate between man and man! I know of nothing that is so deadly as hating somebody. What havoc it sometimes works to the one who is hated! What havoc it always works to the hater! How many an organization has been disrupted by it? How many a church has had its usefulness impaired and the thews of its spiritual strength clipped by it! When given right of way it changes our homes into hells and puts within our hearts that which bites like a serpent and stings like an adder.

How all but infinite has been the cost of hate between section and section, nation and nation! War has certainly been a supreme curse of the world. It is the most deadly foe of mankind. It kills men's bodies, and too often their souls as well. Every war brings in its wake an aftermath of blighted ideals and lowered moral standards. Think of the cost of the World War. Its cost in material wealth was incredibly great. But that was as nothing in comparison with its cost in other directions. It is estimated that its total casualties up to the present time are more than thirty millions of human lives. And so many of them were our choicest and our best.

> Where are you going, Young Fellow, My Lad,
>   On this glittering morn of May?
> I am going to join the colors, Dad,
>   They are wanting men, they say.
> But you are only a boy, Young Fellow, My Lad,
>   You are not obliged to go.
> I'm seventeen and a quarter, Dad,
>   And ever so strong, you know.
>
> So you are off to France, Young Fellow, My Lad?
>   And you are looking so fit and bright.
> I'm dreadfully sorry to leave you, Dad,
>   But I feel that I am doing right.
> God bless you and keep you, Young Fellow, My Lad,
>   For you are all my life, you know.
> Don't worry, I'll soon be back, dear Dad,
>   And I'm awfully proud to go.
>
> What is the matter, Young Fellow, My Lad?
>   No letter again to-day?
> And why did the postman look so sad
>   And sigh as he turned away?
> I hear them say that we've gained new ground,
>   But a terrible price we've paid.

> God grant, my boy, that you are safe and sound,
>   But O, I'm afraid, afraid!
>
> They've told me the truth, Young Fellow, My Lad,
>   And you'll never come home again.
> O God, the dreams and the dreams I've had
>   And the hopes I've nursed in vain!
> For you passed in the night, Young Fellow, My Lad,
>   But you proved in that terrible test,
> Of the bursting shell and the battle hell,
>   That my boy was one of the best.

War is always taking the best, and, taking them, it squanders their lives, so often for nothing and worse than nothing.

C. Finally, we need peacemakers because peace will never come of itself. Peace must be made. We may drift into war. We may drowse and trifle our way into confusion and conflict. But if peace is ever realized it must be through conscious, persistent, sacrificial effort. We must do more than dream of peace; we must make it. And that we can do. Every soul may become a peacemaker. It is impossible for all of us to make fortunes. We cannot all make a great noise in the world. We cannot all make great names. But we can do something far better: we can all make peace, and in so doing invest ourselves for the attaining of the highest possible good.

III

Now, if we are to make peace, how are we to go about it? How is peace to be made? It is not going to be made through hate. That sounds obvious to the point of utter triteness, I know. But, as you turn the pages of history, you will see that it has not been at all obvious, even to the nations that are nominally Christian. Of course we have abandoned to some extent the idea that the way for one neighbor to get along with another is for each to carry a six-shooter. For me to mount a machine gun upon the front porch of the parsonage to defend myself against my neighbors would not be regarded as Christian. That, of course, everybody will recognize.

But somehow we are not so quick to recognize the fact that it is equally unchristian to depend on standing armies and battle ships to keep peace between nation and nation. We readily agree that one Christian cannot hate another, but we are by no means quick in our agreement that Christian nations cannot hate each other. How slow we are in learning that we cannot be Christian individually and pagans nationally! How slow we are in recognizing the obvious truth that we cannot be good Samaritans as individuals and highwaymen and priests and Levites as a nation! We cannot bring about peace between nation and nation by killing each other any more than we can bring it about between man and man.

This, I know, sounds so evident as to seem almost puerile, yet we cannot forget that it has not been long since many of our statesmen and some of our preachers were encouraging us in our fighting by saying that we were waging a war that was to end war. There are multitudes that were honestly convinced that such was the case. They had persuaded themselves that somehow love could be born out of hate and discord, and strife could be the mother of peace. But "do men gather grapes of thorns, or figs of thistles?" "Who can bring a clean thing out of an unclean?" That which is born of love is love, and that which is born of hate is hate. War is an evil, a deadly evil. Hate is an evil. The antidote for this evil is not more evil. Hate is never killed by hate. It is only increased by it. The only successful foe of evil is good.

> For heathen heart that puts her trust
>   In reeking tube and iron shard;
> All valiant dust that builds on dust,
>   And guarding calls not thee to guard:
> For frantic boast and foolish word,
> Thy mercy on thy people, Lord!

How, then, I repeat, are we to become peacemakers? Our first step is putting ourselves into right relations with Jesus Christ. He is the supreme Peacemaker. He is the Prince of Peace. He came to teach us to say, "Our Father," and in so saying to see in every man a brother. He came "to gather together into one the sons of God that are scattered abroad." His last earthly prayer was that we all might be one. He declares that his one great task in the world is the gathering together of men into a brotherhood.

"He that is not for me is against me, and he that gathereth not with me scattereth abroad."

What a startling declaration! Jesus here divides men into two groups. There are those who are for him and those who are against him. There are these two classes and these two only. "Some men," he declares, "enter my service. They make my plans and purposes their plans and purposes. My work becomes their work. They are with me. They struggle to make my dreams into realities. But there are others who oppose me. There are others who fight against me, who antagonize me, who add to the weight of my cross. There are those who by their opposition postpone the coming of that good day when the kingdoms of the world shall become the kingdom of the Lord and his Christ."

In this word also Jesus states with bold emphasis what is the acid test of our loyalty to himself. He declares that all those who make for strife and for discord are arrayed against him. Whoever cherishes hate in his heart, whoever makes it easier for men and women to suspect each other, to mistrust each other, that man, regardless of what his profession may be, is fighting against Christ. Whoever is hard to live with in the home, whoever is a promoter of strife between man and man, whoever makes for discord and misunderstanding within the Church, whoever preaches a patriotism of selfishness, whoever fosters sectional or national or racial prejudices—that man is surely the foe of Jesus Christ. This is true regardless of his claim to loyalty or of his professed orthodoxy. Jesus is come to break down all dividing walls. He is come to abolish unbrotherliness and hate everywhere. If your life and mine are making for the opposite, then we have arrayed ourselves against him whom we claim to serve.

On the other hand, if we are peacemakers, if by what we are and by what we do we preach a gospel of reconciliation, if we make for peace in the home, peace in the social circle, peace between nation and nation and between race and race, then we are making common cause with Jesus Christ. Then we are fighting under his banner. This is true whatever our denomination or lack of it. John brought some great news to Jesus on one occasion. "Master, we saw one casting out demons in thy name." How the heart of Jesus must have leaped for joy! But John had not finished his story. "We forbade him because he followed not with us." What a calamity! "Forbid him not," said Jesus emphatically. "He that is not against us is on our part." Whoever is making for peace in the hearts of men and for peace in the world is a friend and servant of Jesus, and to him we give the right hand of fellowship.

Now, it is through the friends of Jesus that peace is to be made. It is said that a gentleman of saintly life stood one day in a great art gallery before a picture of Jesus. As he looked into the face of him who is the fairest of ten thousand and the one altogether lovely, his heart became strangely warmed and strangely glad. "Bless him, I love him," he said softly to himself. It so happened that there was a man at his side from another nation who overheard his exclamation. "Bless him, I love him too," this man replied. Then there was another and another, till by and by a little group stood reverently about the picture. These represented different nationalities and different races, but they were brought together in the bonds of a sweet and tender brotherhood by their mutual love for Jesus Christ. And one day nation is going to say to nation: "Bless him, we love him." One day the Occident is going to say to the Orient, and the Orient to the Occident: "Bless him, we love him." Then, and not till then, will men beat their swords into plowshares, and their spears into pruning hooks, and learn war no more. Then, and not till then, will the glory of God cover the earth as the waters cover the sea.

What, then, is our first and supreme duty as individuals? If we are to become peacemakers, our first duty is to accept the peace of Christ for ourselves. "He is our peace," Paul tells us. He brings peace between God and man. He brings peace within. That is the first step toward the realization of the great dream of worldwide peace. Have you accepted his peace for yourself? "Peace I leave with you, my peace I give unto you." Let us accept it. If in faith we really receive this peace, we shall come to feel, with the poet:

> God hath given me birth,
> To brother all the sons of earth.

We shall go forth to a ministry of reconciliation. Our appeal will be that of Paul: "Now we are ambassadors for Christ, as though God did beseech you by us; we pray you in Christ's stead, be ye reconciled to God."

9
The First Word from the Cross

Father, forgive them; for they know not what they do (Luke 23:34).

Had you been in Jerusalem on this fateful Friday that changed the world, you would doubtless have been brought under the spell of the excitement of the hour. This excitement was born of the fact that three prisoners were about to pay the death penalty. One of them was a prophet from Nazareth. The other two were revolutionists. The crowd, with a natural love of the gruesome, was hideously eager for the show. This eagerness was doubtless heightened by the fact that all three of the doomed men were well known. This was certainly the case with the prophet. It was probably true of the two outlaws as well.

Not only were all three of these men well known, but they were all popular. The two revolutionists were ardent patriots. Having fought like men, like men they were determined to die. The crowd naturally looked upon them as heroes. The prophet had also been popular. He was so still. This was the case in spite of the fact that most of those immediately surrounding the cross were intensely hostile. So bitter was their antagonism that, having nailed Jesus to the cross, they would not allow him to die in peace. Even the revolutionists, caught under the spell of their bitter antagonism, added their own insults to the senseless howls of the mob and to the cruel jibes of the churchmen. Then something took place that at first silenced one of these revolutionists, then changed his insults into prayers. What happened? The man on the central cross prayed this prayer, "Father, forgive them; for they know not what they do."

I

The fact that the first word that Jesus uttered upon his cross was a prayer does not surprise us. His had been a habit of prayer from his youth. Naturally, he would pray in this black and desperate hour. Even those who refuse to pray when the sea of life is smooth generally refuse no longer when their sea is being whipped by a tempest. There is a sense in which prayer is all but instinctive. When the ground gives way beneath our feet, when some dire tragedy wrenches every visible support from our clinging fingers, we reach for the Unseen almost as naturally as we shrink from a blow. But when we pray under such circumstances, it is almost invariably for ourselves. In our need we cry, "Lord, help me." Nor is there anything wrong in such prayers. We are invited to come boldly to the throne of grace that we may obtain mercy and find grace to help in every time of need. Had Jesus, therefore, thus prayed, it would have been only the natural and the expected.

But what does thrill us is that this first word of prayer that Jesus offered was not for himself. He did not ask for his own deliverance. He did not pray in that black hour for his loved ones, nor for his friends. He prayed for his enemies. He prayed for the soldiers and for the far more cruel churchmen who, having nailed him to the cross, were even then howling about him. It was around the bloody shoulders of these murderers that he flung the folds of this prayer, "Father, forgive them; for they know not what they do."

Once on a certain hill Jesus had preached in this fashion, "Ye have heard that it hath been said, Thou shalt love thy neighbour, and hate thine enemy. But I say unto you, Love your enemies, . . . and pray for them which despitefully use you." On another occasion he had commanded his followers to forgive, not once, but "until seventy times seven"—that is, without limit. Forgiveness was to flow from their hearts as constantly as waters from a gushing spring. What he had preached on the sunny hill of the Sermon on the Mount, he practiced on the grim hill of Calvary. Here he is offering unlimited forgiveness.

II

In asking forgiveness for his murderers Jesus was asking the best possible. This is the case because forgiveness means far more than being let off from a penalty. I am thinking now of a man who committed murder. There was no possible doubt as to his guilt. He was tried and was sentenced to pay the penalty for his crime. But it so happened that he was a man of political influence. He had a heavy claim on the governor of his state. Therefore he was no sooner sentenced then he received a pardon. But in spite of his pardon he still had the stain of blood upon his hands. When God pardons, he does something for us that is far better than merely refusing to punish us as we deserve.

No more is forgiveness a way of escape from the consequences of our wrongdoing. If we sow tares, we are going to reap them, even though we find forgiveness. When David in hot blood had been guilty of adultery, when in cold blood he had committed murder, his faithful minister took his life in his hands and rebuked him for his sin. Then what? David might have come to hate his physician rather than his deadly disease. But he chose the wiser course. As Nathan spoke home to his heart, David's knees went weak, and with a voice choked by sobs he clutched at God's skirts and prayed, "Have mercy upon me." His prayer was not in vain. God heard and answered. He gave to the sinner abundant pardon. But though this forgiveness was full and complete, it did not save David from the terrible consequences of his sin. Instead, he suffered in brokenness of heart to the very end of his days.

A few years ago I went to see a woman who was dying of bichloride of mercury self-administered. She told me of the bitter experience through which she had passed. "At last," she declared, "I felt that I could not bear it any longer. But I am sorry now. I realize that I have done wrong. The reason I have sent for you is to ask you this question, Will God forgive me?"

With complete confidence I answered in the affirmative. I offered her salvation in the name of him who "was wounded for our transgressions." She claimed to accept that salvation, and I feel confident she went to meet her Lord in peace. But there was one something that this forgiveness did not do. It did not take the poison from her tortured body. In spite of the fact that she had been fully forgiven, she died.

What, then, is forgiveness? It is the restoration of a fellowship. When God forgives, he takes us back into his friendship and walks with us as if we had never sinned. He forgets all our ugly past. This is his own promise, "I will forgive their iniquity, and I will remember their sin no more." He treats us as Jesus treated his friends who failed him so miserably in Gethsemane. He had leaned heavily upon these friends. But the best they could do was to go to sleep. More than once he came to wake them, but in spite of all his efforts they threw their big chance away. So what? In spite of their failure we hear our Lord saying to them, "Rise up, let us go." He walked with failures as if they had never failed.

Now since forgiveness means the restoration of a fellowship, it issues in newness of life. As forgiven we thus walk with our Lord, we come more and more to share his divine nature. When, therefore, Jesus prayed for the forgiveness of his enemies, he was asking for them the best possible. He was asking for their regeneration. He was praying that they might experience his fellowship. He was praying that even these murderers might be able to shout with one of the greatest of the saints, "Old things are passed away; behold, all things are become new."

It is significant also that Jesus offered this prayer for the forgiveness of his enemies with complete confidence. He was perfectly sure that full forgiveness was available for every one of them. When he prayed for himself in the garden, he prayed with a condition, an "if" upon his lips, "If it be possible, let this cup pass from me." But here he did not ask the Father to forgive, if forgiveness was possible. He knew that forgiveness was already in his own heart. He knew that what he was offering, God was offering also. Thus Jesus in perfect confidence asked for heaven's best even for his enemies.

III

Then the Master gave a reason why the Father should grant his request: "Forgive them; for they know not what they do." On the surface it seems that Jesus was pleading a palliating circumstance. It was as if he were saying, "These men are doing a terrible wrong, but since they are sinning in ignorance, they are not so guilty as they seem." But this is not what Jesus meant. He was not seeking to excuse their sin. The Bible is never eloquent in making excuses for sin. The individual who does so never wins his way into the presence of God. If you have an excuse for your sin, then you have a right to plead, "Not guilty." But if you dare make such plea, you will never be one inch closer to God than you are now. What, then, did Jesus mean by saying, "They know not what they do"?

He was not affirming that these who were doing him to death did not know that they were doing wrong. Such was not the case. They did know it, every man of them. Pilate, washing his soiled hands, did so in the realization that he had soiled his soul with the stain of a cowardly injustice. Judas, who hurried to empty his soiled hands of the thirty pieces of silver, in order to fill them with a hangman's rope, did so in the consciousness of his guilt. Annas, who had spun his web in the dark, knew that out of greed and envy he had helped to hound a good man to his death. There was not a man of them who with a clean conscience could plead, "Not guilty."

In what sense, then, were they ignorant? They were ignorant in that though they knew that they were doing wrong, they did not and could not realize just how great was their guilt. When Jesus said, "Father, forgive them; for they know not what they do," it was as if he had said, "Forgive them, for they need forgiveness so desperately. Forgive them, for they have committed a sin that is black beyond all their realization." That is doubtless true of every sin we commit. We can never know what harvest we and others may have to reap because of one wrong decision or of one deed of disloyalty.

Thank God, this is also true on its brighter side. We can never know the high use that God can make of one right decision, of one word spoken in loyalty. A young physician called to see me a few years ago. "I became a physician," he declared, "because I knew that as such I would have the privilege of serving others, and as a Christian I was eager to do that." Then he asked, "Do you remember a walk we took together when I was in high school?"

"No," I answered with reluctance.

"Well, I remember it," he replied eagerly. "During that walk you spoke to me about becoming a Christian. As soon as we returned, I went to my room and surrendered to Christ."

What wonderful returns for so small an investment! We can never know, I repeat, the possible triumphant outcome of one right deed. No more can we know the possible tragedy of one wrong deed. Hence this prayer, "Forgive them," for their need was great beyond their knowing.

IV

If this prayer that our Lord offered in perfect confidence for God's best is to be answered for you and me, how are we to make that answer possible?

We must be willing to receive that forgiveness. That we may be willing, we must realize our need. We must come confessing our sin. This is not a rigid rule passed by a narrow-minded God. It is the case in the nature of things. Only those who feel their need of forgiveness will give God a chance. Forgiveness is freely and eagerly offered to every man, but only those who know they have sinned and come short will be willing to accept this offer. Hence our gospel is a gospel for sinners, and for sinners only.

Our Lord enforced this truth by his most fascinating story. A father once prepared a feast to which both his sons were invited. One of these sons was a bit of a renegade, but the other was as decent as decency. While the younger had been a waster, the older had been a worker. When the younger son came home, his garments were stained with the filth of the swine pen. But the older son came with no stain upon him save the innocent soil of the fields. Naturally, this decent chap felt himself unmeasured leagues ahead of his prodigal brother. Not only so, but he had a right so to feel. Yet it was the prodigal who entered the banquet hall while his clean-living, hard-working brother shut the door in his own face.

Why was this the case? It was not because his father cared nothing for decency while he set a premium on profligacy. The door to the feast opened of its own accord to the prodigal because he came with his confession in heart and upon his lips, "I have sinned." That same door was shut in the face of his brother, shut by that brother's own hand, because he came with this confession, "Lo, these many years do I serve thee, neither transgressed I at anytime thy commandment."

There you have it, two confessions: one, "I have *never* sinned"; the other, "I *have* sinned." Which is true? Which is yours? If the former, then you make this prayer of Jesus—this prayer that he offered both by his lips and by his cross—a sheer futility, so far as you are concerned. But if you come with this confession of sin upon your lips, if you come pleading

> Suffice it if—my good and ill unreckoned,
> And both forgiven thro' Thine abounding grace—

then a place at the feast of the fullness of life will be guaranteed to you.

10
The Seventh Word from the Cross

Father, into thy hands I commend my spirit (Luke 23:46).

I

Father, into thy hands I commend my spirit. This is the final word that our Lord uttered from his cross. Not only does this word tell us how Jesus died, but it also tells us how he lived. Charles Lamb wrote of a friend: "Who parted this life on Wednesday evening; dying as he had lived, without much trouble." What Lamb said of his friend is true of mankind in general. As a rule men die as they live. There is nothing in the mere act of passing that makes a bad man good, or a good man bad. Generally we die as we live. So it was with Jesus.

I was reading some years ago of a man who made himself famous in the restaurant business. He established restaurants all the way across our continent. When at last he reached the end of his earthly journey, those nearest to him gathered about his bed to hear his final words. When they bent over him to catch his last whisper, it was this: "Slice the ham thin." There was nothing necessarily wicked about such a final word. It means only that his ruling passion was strong in death.

Not so long ago I was called to see a man who was desperately ill. Though he had largely wasted his substance in riotous living, when he realized that he was coming close to the end, he called for a minister. I went and, in the language of John Wesley, "offered him Christ." Not only so, but I believe that despite the lateness of the hour that offer was accepted. He seemed to receive it with joy, and his loved ones who stood about the bed rejoiced with him. But when a little later he became unconscious and then slipped away, his last word was not a prayer, but an oath. Of course he did not know what he was saying. But so long had he schooled his tongue in the language of blasphemy that he swore spontaneously. Generally speaking, I repeat, we die as we live.

As this is true on the dark side, so it is on the bright. I heard Dr. Edwin McNeill Poteat tell this bit about the home-going of his saintly father, who was also an able minister of the gospel. When this good man realized that he was close to the sunset, he called Edwin McNeill to his bedside and told him of his coming exodus. Then he requested of his son that he conduct his funeral services. "I realize," he continued, "that I am giving you a rather difficult assignment. But," he added, "if you will conduct my services this time, I promise never to ask you to do it again." I like that. So long had this saintly man lived in the fellowship of his Lord that he could even face death with a twinkle in his eye. Thus he died as he lived, in joyful confidence.

II

"Father, into thy hands I commend my spirit." As this word sums up the death of Jesus, so, I repeat, it sums up his life. As his robe was woven of one piece, so also his life was of one piece. There was no break between his living and his home-going. To be convinced of this we need only to turn afresh to the pages of the New Testament. Here we see that what Jesus did in his final moments he had been doing throughout the years.

A. In this word, "Father, into thy hands I commend my spirit," Jesus is quoting from the thirty-first psalm. In his final hour he turned to the hymnbook of his people. But this turning to the scriptures was nothing new in the life of our Lord. This was not the first time since he had come to the cross that he made use of this book. His cry of dereliction, though so fully his own that we tend to forget that it was first uttered by lesser lips, is also a quotation from the Psalms. In fact our Lord had so saturated his mind and heart with the Bible that both its thought and its language became his own.

For instance, when people came to him with questions, he would often ask, "Have ye not read?" or, "How readest thou?" When a certain lawyer asked him to tell what was the supreme commandment, Jesus did not express an opinion of his own; he simply referred his questioner to the Old Testament. On another occasion the Sadducees, who did not believe in the resurrection, and who accepted only the first five books of the Bible, came to him with this rather comical story: There were seven brothers who, from the oldest to the youngest, had consecutively married a certain woman. Now, since they all married her, this was the question: If there is a resurrection, whose wife is she going to be? Personally, I have never felt that there would be any great contest for her. But that is not the point. The point is that Jesus answered that part of their story that had to do with the resurrection with a quotation from the book of Exodus.

As Jesus used the Bible for the instruction of others, even so he made use of it in the living of his own life. When I visited Mount Vernon, I was interested in the sword with which Washington armed himself during the Revolutionary War. The Old Testament was the sword of the Spirit with which Jesus fought his battles. Every onslaught of the enemy during his struggle in the wilderness he repelled by a thrust of this keen blade. It was only natural, therefore, that Jesus in his last hour should turn afresh to the book that had been his constant companion through his entire life. There was about it a beautiful spontaneity.

B. This word is a prayer. Jesus did not use the exact words of the scriptures. He added one word of his own. That was "Father." As our Lord had made a habit of saturating his mind with the Bible, so he had made a habit of prayer. He had taught men to pray by what he said. He had taught them also by what he did. In fact if we take the Gospels as our guide, we discover that the only work that ever really taxed the energies of Jesus was the work of prayer. After he prayed, everything else seemed to come as a matter of course. From the place of prayer he went as a victor to receive the spoils of his conquest. Having thus practiced prayer day by day, Jesus found it perfectly natural to pray as he reached the end of his journey.

C. This prayer was an act of dedication. It was a committal.

Moffatt gives this translation: "I trust my spirit to thy hands." This committal of himself to God was also a habit of Jesus. His Bible reading and prayer helped to this end. "I consecrate myself," is a part of the last prayer that he prayed with his disciples. Always he could say, "The Father hath not left me alone because I do always the things that please him." After he had made the commitment of himself to his Father a fixed habit of his life, it was only natural for him to fall asleep with this prayer upon his lips, "Father, into thy hands I commend my spirit."

III

"Father, into thy hands I commend my spirit." As these words sum up what both life and death meant to Jesus, they also sum up what they ought to mean to us. If we make this committal to God the habit of our lives, then we may be sure that such habit will stand us in good stead, both when we are in the thick of the fight and when we come to the end of our earthly journey. "I trust my spirit to thy hands." This is the whole meaning of our Christian religion. This is the least we can do and be Christian at all. It is the most we can do, either in time or in eternity.

A. Committal is the doorway into the kingdom. How do we become Christians? Our experiences are varied since God is a God of variety. We do not all react in the same fashion. But there are characteristics of conversion that are common to all of us. They are obedience, surrender, dedication. We enter by the door of commitment because there is none other.

Take Paul, for instance. When we read these thrilling words: "I saw in the way a light from heaven, above the brightness of the sun, shining round about me and them which journeyed with me," we say, "Of course Paul was converted after an experience like that. If I were to see such splendor in my sky, I too would be converted." But this would not necessarily be the case.

Paul might have gone from the brightness of the light of this vision into a deeper darkness than he had ever known before. This vision no more saved Paul than the sight of a laughing spring would save a man who was dying of thirst. Before the thirsty man can be saved, he must kiss the spring on the lips. Before Paul could be saved, he had to obey. He sums up his secret in one single sentence: "I was not disobedient unto the heavenly vision." The great apostle therefore entered the kingdom through the door of committal.

There was another apostle whose conversion was just as real as that of Paul. Yet how commonplace his story seems! "As Jesus passed . . . , he saw a man, named Matthew, sitting at the receipt of custom: and he saith unto him, Follow me." Then what? We read the answer in this simple sentence: "And he arose, and followed him." Did he pray? Did he laugh? Did he sob? Did he shout and sing? We are not told. We are told only that he obeyed. He made a committal of himself. Thus he entered the kingdom.

That is the door that we must enter, for there is none other. Here was a lovely young aristocrat who was a far finer man than Matthew. He had almost everything in his favor. He was clean, courageous, and religious. Yet when Jesus gave him the same invitation that he gave to Matthew, when he said, "Follow me," the young ruler did not make the same response. Instead we read of him this tragic word, "He went away." He missed entering the kingdom, not because he was bad, but because he refused to make a committal of himself.

B. Not only is obedience the door into the kingdom, but it is the life of the kingdom. When the author of the book of Genesis undertakes to tell us what life meant to Enoch, he puts it in a single sentence: "Enoch walked with God." One day Enoch stretched a groping hand into the encircling gloom, and that almighty hand that is always feeling for yours and mine in the daylight and dark found the hand of Enoch, and he thus became acquainted with God. After he met God, nothing else seemed quite so worthwhile as to walk with him. But how did this acquaintance ripen into friendship? The writer to the Hebrews answers that question: "He had this testimony, that he pleased God." That is, he walked with God through daily obedience.

So it was with Paul. When he first met Jesus, he surrendered to him. He died to his own will and to his own way. But that one death was not enough. Paul affirms, "I die daily." Every day he died afresh. He died to his own plans and purposes that he might make his own the plans and purposes of his Lord. It was this daily dying that enabled him to pass from the "these things" of his conversion to the "those things" of an ever-growing Christian experience.

C. "Father, I trust my spirit to thy hands." This is what the Bible means by perfection. If it is the least I can do and be a

Christian, it is also the most I can do either in time or in eternity. In fact, if I do this, nothing else is required. This puts us all on an equal footing. There are a thousand things that you can do that I cannot. I can do some things that you cannot. But we can all do God's best. We can give ourselves to him. That is not only good, in the mind of our Lord; it is perfection.

IV

"Father, I trust my spirit to thy hands." Since this is all God asks of us, what ought we to do about it?

A. We ought to make full committal of ourselves in the here and now. We are to make this committal not because it is a small and easy matter. When Paul beseeches us to present our bodies, our very selves, to God, he does not encourage us to do this because it will cost us nothing. On the contrary, it will cost us everything. We are to give in the faith that what we give he will accept. Let us therefore give ourselves to God with the assurance that he will gladly accept us.

B. Let us dedicate ourselves to God in the faith that what he accepts he remakes. I read of a great artist who was spending a few days in a humble home. It so happened that while he was a guest the little girl of the family had a birthday. Among the presents she received was a silk fan. It was a fairly ordinary affair, but when she showed it to the artist he said, "If you will let me keep this for a little while, I will paint you a picture on it."

But she snatched it away, saying, "You shan't spoil my fan."

If she had only trusted him, he would have given it back with its beauty and worth increased a thousandfold. Give yourself to God, and more and more he will transform you into the image of his glory.

C. Give yourself to God, and he will use you. He may not always use you in the way of your own choosing. He may not always lead you in green pastures beside still waters. He will not always use you in a fashion to make you comfortable. In using his own Son in the finest possible fashion he could not permit him to by-pass Calvary. As he uses you, you may become increasingly acquainted with the Cross. But use you he will.

D. Finally, if you give yourself to God, not only will he accept, transform, and use you, but he will walk with you to the very end. I am quite sure that the Good Shepherd who has been with his sheep during the sunny days will not leave them at nightfall when they need him most. I have no slightest envy of the man who is master of his fate and captain of his soul. I have no desire to venture into life alone, nor do I dare face eternity alone. But if I pray with my Lord this prayer, "I trust my spirit to thy hands," I can face both today and tomorrow without fear.

11
God's Plan for my Life

I have finished the work which thou gavest me to do (John 17:4).

These are the words of Jesus as He stood at the end of the way. Life now lay behind Him. Its battles have been fought. Its victories have been won. There was before Him yet only the tragedy of Calvary, but as He had already got the consent of His own will to pass through this, He counted this victory as achieved. He is already within the shadow of the Cross. His foot is upon the threshold of death. As a mountain climber might look back from the summit of the mountain over the way along which he had struggled upward, so Jesus stops upon the height of the mountain of life and looks back.

As He looked back He was not disappointed. As He looked back He was satisfied. There were no weeds along the way that He had planted that He would like now to pluck up. There were no flowers that He might have sown along the way that were left unplanted. The book of His life's story was a finished book. He had no corrections to make, no unkind thrusts to rub out, no love words to write in. It was finished.

And by its being finished, it does not mean simply that Jesus had reached the end of His life. We all do that. In the far north a skeleton was found seated at the root of a tree, and up above his head was a carved finger pointing to it with these words: "This is the end of the trail." And the poor dying fellow, with his goal unreached and with his ambition unrealized, had come thus far and could go no farther, and so he carved this pathetic word and sat down and died: "This is the end of the trail."

But when Christ says, "I have finished the work" He claims that the task has not simply been ended, but it has been perfected. He claims that He has lived the one flawless, the one complete, the one perfect life that this world has ever seen. That it is perfect no man will deny. It has endured the scrutiny of nineteen centuries, and the verdict of friend and foe still is that of perplexed and bewildered Pilate, "I find no fault in Him at all.'

Now, what is the secret of the life of Jesus? First, it does not grow out of the fact, as some seem to believe, that Jesus was divine. Christ emptied Himself, the Apostle tells us. So when He met temptation, He met it as a man. And when He worked miracles, He worked them as a man. And when He wrought His marvelous ministry, He did it through the same spiritual power that is available for all men.

The secret of the life of Jesus is summed up in this: "I came not to do mine own will, but the will of Him that sent me." The biography of Jesus was written in the mind and heart of God. And Jesus, by His absolute surrender to the will of God, made God's plan an actuality. In every step of His life He realized and recognized God's plan and God's leadership. Again and again He refers to His hour, meaning by that that the index finger that points to the time at which He is to act is that of no human hand, but the hand of His Father. This was the secret of His continued enjoyment of His Father's companionship. "He that hath sent me is with me. The Father hath not left me alone, for I do always the things that please Him." The life of Jesus was God-planned, and Jesus found that plan and lived it. And that is the secret of the beauty and power of that life that has held the world in its grip all through the centuries.

But no more truly did God plan the life of Jesus Christ than He plans your life and mine. I know of no truth that is more thrilling than this, that has more power to lift us upon our feet in joyous and expectant hopefulness. We are not here by accident. We are not here as creatures of chance. We are here on a definite mission of our Father's own choosing. I know that infidelity and heathenism laugh at the idea. I know that paganism voices its belief in that pathetic sentence:

> And fear not lest Existence closing your
> Account, and mine, should know the like no more;
> The Eternal Saki from that Bowl hath pour'd
> Millions of Bubbles like us, and will pour.
>
> When you and I behind the Veil are past,
> Oh, but the long, long while the World shall last,
> Which of our Coming and Departure heeds
> As the Sea's self should heed a pebble-cast.

But God lets us know that we are not so many useless and unnoticed bubbles, but worthful human souls, each with a definite mission, each one unique. There was never another individual just like you. There never will be in all the eternities. In the springtime God sows a million flowers and hangs a million verdant banners upon the boughs of the trees, but there are no two alike. "Whenever God makes a man He breaks the mold." Every man has his own individuality and his own special mission. God was in earnest when He made you because you can be and do something for Him that no other human soul can be and do.

Why do we say that God plans every life? In the first place, we say it because He plans everything else in this universe. No man can look open-eyed into the face of nature without realizing that back of nature, and within it, is a planning purposeful God. The very flowers tell the story in words of perfume and color. I look at the lily's magic garments. Where did it get its living dress? Not from the wardrobe of Solomon. Earth's kings have no such garments. The lily—why God clothed it. He wove its white dress out of sunbeams and dewdrops and the mysteries of the soil. And nobody can weave such garments but God.

I listen to the song of the mockingbird and the canary. Where did those birds go to school? Who taught them music? Ah, you know. Those little birds sing the songs that their Master taught them, notes caught from the Choir Invisible. Who made the calendar for the swallow? How does it know when the snows are coming? Who made his geography? Who drew the map of that far away country where the roses bloom all the year and where spring never takes vacation? Who gave him his compass and blazed the trail to these unknown summer lands? Ah, you know—

> There is a power whose care
> Guides thy way along that trackless coast,
> The desert and the illimitable air,
> Lone, wandering, but not lost.
> And—He who from zone to zone guides
> Through the trackless heavens thy solemn flight,
> In the long way that I must tread alone,
> Will guide my steps aright.

Not only does the world about us tell us the story of a planning God, but the great worlds above us have the same message. The Psalmist tells us how that one day he went to church. His pew, I suppose, was one of the Judean hills. The preacher was the heavens, and the theme of his sermon was the glory of God. He told us about it in a wonderful song that he wrote: "The heavens declare the glory of God and the firmament showeth his handiwork." And Addison attended that same church centuries later and wrote:

> The spacious firmament on high,
> With all the blue ethereal sky,
> And spangled heavens, a shining frame,
> Their great Original proclaim.
> The unwearied sun, from day to day,
> Does his Creator's power display,
> And publishes to every land
> The work of an almighty hand.
>
> Soon as the evening shades prevail,
> The moon takes up the wondrous tale,
> And nightly, to the listening earth,
> Repeats the story of her birth;
> While all the stars that round her burn,
> And all the planets in their turn,
> Confirm the tidings as they roll,
> And spread the truth from pole to pole.
>
> What though in solemn silence all
> Move round the dark terrestrial ball?
> What though no real voice nor sound
> Amid the radiant orbs be found?
> In reason's ear they all rejoice,
> And utter forth a glorious voice;
> Forever singing as they shine,
> "The hand that made us is divine."

God has millions of trains flying through the trackless distances of space, but not one of them has ever been late by a fraction of a second in all the centuries. Now, if God plans the flowers and birds and stars, I believe He also plans your life and mine. For when the last flower is withered and the last bird song dead and the last star has closed its silvery eye, you and I shall be yet in our infancy in the great Nursery of Eternity.

I believe God plans our lives, in the second place, because it is the clear teaching of His Book. As we turn the pages of our Bible we find man after man whose life God definitely planned. And these lives are victorious and useful, just in proportion as they are loyal to the will of God. And when they take themselves outside the circle of His will there is always failure and disappointment. What a pathetic ruin is Saul! I know of few pictures more tragic than the poor, dogged and perplexed man as he wakes up to his utter godlessness. Hear his pathetic sob: "The Lord has departed from me and heareth me no more!" What is the secret of his ruin? Disobedience—he took himself out of the hand of God.

Not only does our Lord teach us this through the lives of His saints, He also teaches it by very unmistakable declarations. He said that "He gave to every man his work." He said, "As the Father hath sent me, even so send I you." We see Him definitely choosing men for discipleship. We see Him sending out Barnabas and Paul on their first missionary tour. And we see all through the centuries men and women by the thousand who have gone forth to live their lives under the conscious leadership of the Spirit of God—men and women who were enabled to say: "To this end was I born and for this cause came I into the world."

Now, what does it mean for God to plan our lives? Certainly it is a truth that ought to let loose a whole choir of songbirds in our hearts. It ought to sow a very profusion of flowers in the garden of our souls. This is true because it speaks of the highest possible privilege. For, mark you, God's planning our lives does not mean that He has fixed a groove in which we must run whether we want to or not. It simply means this, that God has planned and we may or may not execute the plan. Remember God will never compel you to accept His will for your life. You may tear His plans into shreds. Just as many a young fellow has thwarted the plans of those who love him, so you may thwart the plans and purposes of God in your life.

No, this doctrine does not mean compulsion. It means privilege, and that only. It means that God is the architect and man is the builder. You may refuse His plans, but in so doing you have refused the highest. In so doing you deliberately uncrown yourself. In so doing you miss the deepest and sweetest secret of human blessedness. For the secret of life at its best is just this, to live it within the circle of the will of God.

Now, the supreme question, it seems to me, especially for you young people, is just this: What is God's will for my life? What did God mean when He made me? What purpose does He have in me?

"To be or not to be, that is the question?" But if question it is, it is the question of the stage. It is the question of a mad man. It is the question of a pessimist. It is the question of one in hopeless rebellion and despair at the fact that the world is out of joint and that he was ever born to set it right.

But the question for men and women, sons and daughters of God, is this: Being, how shall I make the most of life? How shall I meet my obligations and discharge my responsibilities in the finest and noblest way? And there is but one answer to that question—you will come to your highest only as you find and carry out in your own life God's purpose for you. He knows you as you can never know yourself. To enter into His will is to climb the mountain heights of your highest possibilities.

But how am I to know God's will for me? There are a number of considerations, I think, that enter into the solution of this question. Of course there are some things we know that are true of all of us in general. We know that our part at least is to be a part of helping and not of hindering. It is to be a part of serving and not simply of being served. It is to be a part of going forward and not of holding back, of lifting up and not of dragging down. There are some people who seem to think that all they were sent here to do is to stand on the side line and watch the game and criticise the players. But God never called any man to any such low and unholy calling.

How am I to know? In the first place, I think you may be guided in some measure by your own talents, by your aptitude. Other things being equal, I believe God calls a man to do what he can do.

Second, you will be influenced in some measure by the work that needs to be done. What does life need? Where is the field whose ripening harvests promise the largest returns from the investment of a life? Where do I see the opening of the widest door? For, believe me, today doors are opening everywhere. God is needing men in business who will conduct their business as Christian stewards. God is needing men in professional life who will discharge their professions as ministers of the manifold grace of God. In this great field of the world where God so needs laborers, what is the loudest call that comes to me?

And then finally, God has promised you His personal guidance in the selection of your life task. "In all thy ways acknowledge Him and He shall direct thy path." If you will ask God to lead you into the realization of His plan and purpose for you, ask Him with a willingness to follow where He leads, He will not disappoint you. I do not say He will give you a map of the whole way, but He will show you the task that comes first, and He will enable you to sing:

> Keep thou my feet; I do not ask to see
> The distant scene; one step enough for me.

And whether your life is lived in the throng or in the obscure place, whether it is to be a ministry packed with service or a ministry of hidden pain, whether you are a Knight of the Sick Room or a hero of the field of battle—God will guide you and will give you the glad consciousness that you are in your place and are fulfilling the good and acceptable and perfect will of God.

What would it mean for us this morning, if definitely and with wholeness of heart we should put our lives into God's hands for the fulfilling of His purposes? It would mean for some of us the changing of the plans that we have made for ourselves. It would mean for some the giving up of our selfish ambitions. It would mean for some, a definite decision for the Christian ministry. How the Church is needing preachers today, and what a field it is! To what greater honor could any man aspire than to the high position of being a preacher of the "unsearchable riches of Christ!" Paul said he was poor—and poor he was, but that he made many rich. What a fine task to enrich the world, to find men poor in hope, poor in power, poor in the presence of the devastations that death has wrought, and to leave them rich, rich in the confidence that God is able to save unto the uttermost, rich in the glorious assurance that one day "this corruptible must put on incorruption" and that love shall find its own in the Land of Eternal Sunshine.

What finer ambition could any mother have for her boy than that he should be a minister of the Gospel of Christ? And how you might help him in his decision if you would but talk with him and pray for him! For the homes where preachers are called and the homes where missionaries are called are homes whose religious life is made vital and warm by the breath of prayer. "The harvest truly is plenteous and the laborers are few." Ask the Lord to send you. Ask the Lord to send the child of your love into the Christian ministry to serve God here in the great and romantic enterprise of helping to bring in the Kingdom by the preaching of the Gospel.

If you will yield yourself to God today it might mean for some of you that God would call you to be missionaries. The money has been pledged in our great Centenary enterprise, but we are needing more missionaries and more preachers, more young men and women to give themselves to special and definite Christian work. To what finer enterprise could you dedicate your life than to that of witnessing for God in the faraway places of the earth? We must overcome the evils of heathenism with good or we ourselves shall be conquered, for we are one world as never before. There are "no wards in this world hospital" today. We are all together. The only way that we can remain vitally Christian ourselves is to give Christianity to the nations.

To submit yourself definitely to the will of God would mean for most of us the doing of the same tasks that we are doing, but the doing of them in a new and glorious spirit. For the will of God transfigures every task, however low, and floods it with the light of eternity. God is calling most of us to serve in the places that are humble and obscure, but if we are faithful we shall as genuinely carry out His purpose as the mightiest archangel before His throne.

> Thousands at His bidding speed and post
> O'er hand and ocean without rest;
> They also serve, who only stand and wait.

The big question for all of us is just this: "Lord, what wilt thou have me do?" Have you found the answer to that question?

We must be willing to go or to stay, as God shall call. Sometimes those that long to stay in the home field are strangely driven forth by the will of God. Sometimes those who wish to go are just as strangely held back. Many a time these ways of God are perplexing and we do not understand. However, I am sure that one day, if not here, at least when we look back upon our road from some watch tower in eternity, we shall understand fully.

I bring you to this question: What are you going to do with your life? How many men I have known who looked back with regret! Some of them were called into the ministry and refused. Some of them were called to give their lives to noble and unselfish service and refused. Today they look back over it all with grief too bitter for tears.

Dr. F. B. Meyer tells this story. A young man stepped into the study of his uncle one morning. That uncle was a great preacher. He said to him, "Uncle, what are you going to preach about Sunday?" And the preacher replied, "I am going to preach on this text: 'To this end was I born, and for this cause came I into the world.'" The young man was thoughtful for a moment and said, "Uncle, why was I born?" And the preacher replied, "I do not know, but if you will be obedient God will let you know."

The young man left the room and went out on the street. Just around the corner he saw a crowd before a theater. He hurried to the scene and found that the building was in flames. He assisted in the work of rescue. He brought out one man after another till he had saved some thirteen. He was then struck by a piece of falling timber and taken in a state of unconsciousness to the hospital. Word was carried to his uncle and he hurried to the hospital to see him. As the preacher entered the room where the wounded man lay he opened his eyes. Consciousness had come back to him, just a brief moment of consciousness before he passed into the presence of the King. And he said, "Uncle, I know now 'to this end was I born and for this cause came I into the world' that I might save those thirteen."

That preacher said that months later he was in a hotel in Paris. A wild eyed man approached him and began to talk. He grew more and more excited in his talk. At last he said, "I was in a burning building sometime ago and I saved myself. I saved myself!" Just then a man came and led him away. A little later this man returned to apologize to the preacher. He said, "This man was in a theater that burned some months ago. He left his friends and saved himself, and the thought of it has driven him mad."

There is only one sure road to your highest usefulness. There is only one way to realize your highest blessedness, and that is in the doing of the will of God. To seek to save your life is to lose it. To lose your life is to keep it unto life eternal. May the Lord grant unto us so to live that when the sunset comes we may be able in our finite way to say, "I have glorified thee on the earth. I have finished the work which thou gavest me to do."

12
The Forks of the Road—Moses

By faith Moses, when he was come to years, refused to be called the son of Pharaoh's daughter; choosing rather to suffer affliction with the people of God, than to enjoy the pleasures of sin for a season; esteeming the reproach of Christ greater riches than the treasures in Egypt: for he had respect unto the recompense of the reward (Heb. 11:24-26).

I

Moses is at the forks of the road. A very revealing place is this spot where the roads fork. Here every man shows himself for what he is. One man comes to the forks of the road and undertakes to stand perfectly still. He is afraid to turn either to the right hand or to the left lest he go wrong. Or he travels the road to the left for a season, then retraces his steps and for another season travels the road to the right. Such conduct indicates that he is afflicted with the fatal malady of indecision. When Moses comes to the forks of the road he refuses the one and sets himself steadfastly to travel the other. By so doing he shows himself a man of decision.

II

There were two elements in this decision of Moses, as there are in all decisions.

A. There was a negative element. "Moses when he was come to years refused." That is, there was something to which Moses said "No." And, mark you, his "No" was a full-fledged, one hundred per cent negative. It was not tinctured with a single ounce of "Yes." So often when we say "No" it is lacking in positiveness. Likewise, when we say "Yes," there is a weakness about it that indicates an admixture of the negative. Moses, when he stood at the forks of the road, looked at both roads, and to one of them he said a positive, vigorous, out and out "No."

B. But Moses did more than say "No." He did something more than refuse to take a certain road. He also said "Yes." He refused to travel one way, not that he might stand still, but that he might travel another way. So often we content ourselves with a mere refusal. When we hear the call of Christ almost the first thought that comes into our mind is not that to which we are to say "Yes," but that to which we are to say "No." We think of the Christian life on its negative side rather than on its positive side. We think of what we are to quit being and doing rather than what we are to become and what we are to do.

Now, it is altogether right to remember that certain things must be given up in order for us to become followers of Jesus Christ. But we must also remember this: That no amount of negatives will make us Christians. No man ever becomes a Christian by virtue of what he does not do. No amount of "don'ts" summed up will equal a saint, as no amount of ciphers summed up will equal a unit. Therefore, it is the poorest possible plea, when we respond to Christ's call to become disciples by enumerating the wicked things that we do not do. It is necessary to be able to say "No." But to simply say "No" and stop there is to end in utter moral failure.

There is a handsome wax figure in one of the stores on Main Street. When I approached him and told him where he could get a case of bootleg liquor, he refused to be interested. When I told him where he could bet on a sure thing, he was also indifferent. When I sought to amuse him with a smutty story, he had the decency not to be amused. When I complimented his competitor on the opposite side of the street, he did not turn green with envy. To every temptation he said a very positive "No." But when encouraged by his refusals to do the wrong, I invited him to prayer meeting, he was as unresponsive as the average church member. And when I passed the collection plate, he did not even see it. Therefore, I cannot call this gentlemanly wax figure a Christian. He is as far from being a saint as death is far from life.

The truth of the matter is that Christ is calling on you to say "No" not simply because he wants you to practice self-denial as an end. He is calling on you to say "No" to the lower because that is absolutely necessary in order for you to say "Yes" to the highest. He is asking you to say "No" to the darkness because in no other way can you say "Yes" to the light. He is asking you to say "No" to the mud puddle in order that you may say "Yes" to the infinite sea. He is asking you to say "No" to the ant hill in order that you may say "Yes" to the majestic mountain. He is asking you to say "No" to sin in order that you may say "Yes" to righteousness. He is asking you to say "No" to uselessness in order that you may say "Yes" to usefulness. He is asking you to say "No" to the Devil in order that you may say "Yes" to Himself.

III

This decision of Moses was costly.

A. There was much to be given up.

1. This decision involved the giving up of the highest social position in all the land of Egypt. It was to pass in one step from this high position, not to a lower rank, but to the very lowest. It was to cease to be the son of the Egyptian princess in order to become the son of a Hebrew slave. And, mark you, social position is not a thing that we despise. There are people that are willing to pay almost any price to win and retain a high social standing. I have seen mothers willing to give their pure and tender daughters to dance with men that they knew to be libertines just in order to get them into society. When, therefore, Moses said "No" to this high social position, he said "No" to something that makes a tremendous appeal to the average man and woman.

2. When Moses made this decision, he said "No" to the pleasures of Egypt. The Egypt of that day was the New York of modern life. It was the playground of the world. Here every pleasure could be enjoyed, from the most fastidious and refined to the most bestial and vulgar. All these pleasures were within

reach of the hand of Moses. And, therefore, when he said "No," he rejected all that could appeal to a man who was in love with worldly pleasure.

3. His decision involved the giving up of the treasures of Egypt. The Egypt of that day was the granary of the world. Down from its unknown source every year came the Nile, giving to Egypt its fertility. To Egypt came the ships and caravans of many nations, carrying away her grain and leaving behind their silver and gold. Much of this treasure went into the coffers of Pharaoh. When Moses, therefore, said "No" to the treasures of Egypt, he refused to grip and hold vast wealth that might have been his for the taking.

4. For Moses to make this decision was to bring bitter disappointment to one who loved him, and to whom he was under very great obligations. I think we have never given sufficient credit to this Egyptian princess who was Moses' foster mother. The fact that she was a heathen did not prevent her from being a good woman. It did not rob her of a mother heart. When that strange craft afloat on the Nile was found, and when its lone occupant pelted this Egyptian princess with his weakness and cannonaded her with his tears, she had the grace and the tenderness to capitulate. She took this little waif to her heart and protected him. It was to her that he owed his life. It was to her that he owed the fact that he had been educated in the royal universities. It was by no means easy, therefore, for a big-souled man like Moses to disappoint one who had thus helped him and who tenderly loved him.

B. But the cost of this decision of Moses is not to be measured alone by what he gave up. What he chose in place of it all was also costly. When he refused all that Egypt had to offer, what did he accept in its stead? When he said "No" to the privileges that might have been his as the son of Pharaoh's daughter, to what did he say "Yes"?

He chose suffering. "Moses, when he was come to years, refused to be called the son of Pharaoh's daughter, choosing rather to suffer affliction with the people of God." This is an arresting statement. Here is a man facing a road that he knows will lead him to suffering, to agony, to disappointment, to battle and conflict and tears. Yet, with his eyes wide open, he makes the choice. He does not dream for a moment that when he identifies himself with a horde of slaves he is going to have an easy time. He does not fool himself into believing that the course upon which he has decided will be all sunshine and all laughter. He knows that there will be battles to fight. He knows that there will be heavy burdens to be borne. He knows that there will be many a misunderstanding and many a disappointment and many a heartache. Yet, with his eyes wide open, and alive to all that is involved, he chooses to suffer affliction with the people of God.

IV

How did Moses come to make this choice?

A. He had a clear eye for distinguishing right from wrong. How easy it is for us to persuade ourselves that the thing we want to do is the thing we ought to do! How easy it would have been for Moses to have accepted the career that was open to him as the son of Pharaoh's daughter! He might have reminded himself of the large service rendered by Joseph. Joseph had saved his people in the past not by descending, but by ascending. Joseph had become prime minister of Egypt. He himself might have promised a kindred salvation by keeping his position as the son of Pharaoh's daughter. But he refused to let his own interests blind him. He saw that to cling to his rights would be to sin. He refused to blind himself to the fact that it was not simply sinful to choose the lowest, it was also sinful to choose the second best. He realized that God was calling him to choose the highest and to fail to so choose was to sin.

B. He knew that the pleasures and gains of sin are only temporary. Sin is only charming in the present or in the immediate future. It has no charm in the past. How fascinating is sin a moment before it is committed! How absolutely necessary it seems to our happiness! But when it slips into the past its pearly teeth become ugly fangs, its shapely hands become unshapely claws, its winsome tresses become writhing serpents. The sin of the future often seems as fair as an angel from heaven, but the sin of yesterday is as ugly as a fiend from hell.

What a pity that we do not have this clear insight possessed by Moses. He faced the fact that there were pleasures in sin. The Bible everywhere confesses that fact. Sin has its laughter and its song and its sunshine. Sin has its pleasures, but they do not last.

Its most brilliant career soon comes to an end. Its brightest day soon closes. Its sweetest draught is soon drunk. Its fairest flowers are soon faded. Choose the way of sin if you will, and though you may laugh, your laughter will be but temporary. Though you may rejoice, your joy will be as fleeting as a shadow. Then one day when the laughter has all died and your roses are all withered and your songs are all hushed, you will have a whole eternity in which to curse yourself.

C. He had a keen eye for the things of real value. So clearly did he see, that he esteemed the reproach of Christ greater riches than the treasures of Egypt. It took a man deeply schooled in permanent values to reach that conclusion. The treasures of Egypt loomed large. They seemed very genuine and very weighty and very abiding. The reproach of Christ—how uninviting! How lacking in winsomeness! Yet Moses decided that the thing of real value was not the wealth of Egypt, but the reproach of Christ. What a seeing eye did this man possess!

D. Then Moses looked away from everything else to the coming reward. He believed that the future belongs not to sin but to righteousness. He believed it is the heritage, not of the holders of the treasures of Egypt, but of those who share the reproach of Christ. He refused to allow temporary gain to blind him to the gain that is eternal. He looked away from everything else to the coming reward. He looked away from Egypt's splendor and power. He looked away from Egypt's molehills and ant heaps to the majestic mountains that loomed in the hazy distance. His faith gave him at once the far view and the true view. "He had respect unto the recompense of the reward."

V

And what was the outcome of this decision?

A. Moses received the reward of a Christlike character. Do you see that man coming down from the mountain with face that is strangely alight? Do you find your eyes dazzled in his presence as if you were looking upon a sunrise? Whose is the face that must needs have a veil to cover it before we can look upon it? It is the face of a man who refused the treasures of Egypt and chose the reproach of Christ. The splendor of his face has not come to him from long gazing upon silver and gold. Such a gaze hardens the face and darkens all its radiance. Whence, then, came this winsome light? It has come from looking upon God. Had Moses remained in Egypt he would have missed many a conflict and struggle. He would also have missed a face lighted with the light that shines in the face of Jesus Christ.

B. Through this decision Moses was able to render a great service to his own nation and to the world. "Whose are those white tents in the valley?" I ask him one day. "They are the tents of God's chosen people, Israel," he answers. "Israel?" I reply in amazement. "I thought Israel was in bondage. I thought her people were slaves. I thought they were giving themselves solely to the task of brick making." "They were," he replies, "till I came. But by the grace of God I have led them from bondage to freedom."

But I am in doubt as to whether Moses' service in freeing his people has been greatly worthwhile. They are such a peevish and fretful and whining lot. They are forever lusting for the flesh pots of Egypt. They are constantly complaining to Moses because he has not left them to die in the land of bondage. I cannot convince myself that his task has been worth the doing. So I speak my mind:—"Pardon me, Moses. You have made a heroic fight. You have set your people free. But they are a cantankerous lot, and I fear your labor has been almost, if not quite, in vain."

But Moses does not seem to share my doubts. "Israel does not count for much now," he replies, "but remember that he is only a child. He has by no means arrived, but he is on the way. You may not believe it, but he will yet render the world a great service. One day he is going to write a Book, and that book will do more than all other books to banish the world's wrongs and the world's night and to bring in a reign of righteousness. One day he is going to give to the world an Isaiah with his inspired eloquence, and a Jeremiah with his broken heart and his streaming tears. One day he is going to give to the world a skylark named David and a flaming missionary named Paul. One day there is going forth from his little country the best of all good news:— 'Behold, I bring you glad tidings of great joy, for there is born unto you this day a Saviour, which is Christ the Lord.' Israel does not count for much yet. But he is on the way toward bringing the whole world into his debt."

C. Then, incidentally, this decision enabled Moses to win heaven. The New Testament makes us sure of this. Read the story of the Transfiguration. Christ has come. He is struggling under the burden of his coming Cross. He needs help such as those deeply schooled in the mystery of suffering alone can give. Therefore, two men, passed from earth long years ago, came to talk with Him of His coming crucifixion. Who are they? One of them is the man who esteemed the reproach of Christ greater riches than the treasures of Egypt. Whence does he come? The One to whom he speaks, his own shining face, the whole story, answers that question. He comes from heaven. He is fresh from the house of many mansions. There he had been for long centuries. And there he is at this hour, glad with the joy of those who are forever with the Lord.

We must conclude, therefore, that the best day's work that Moses ever did was when he made possible the writing of this sentence:—"By faith Moses, when he was come to years, refused to be called the son of Pharaoh's daughter; choosing rather to suffer affliction with the people of God than to enjoy the pleasures of sin for a season; esteeming the reproach of Christ greater riches than the treasures of Egypt: for he had respect unto the recompense of the reward." He gave up the passing and the temporal, but he won the wealth that endures. He won Christlike character. He won abiding usefulness. He won an inheritance among that elect company who "have washed their robes and made them white in the blood of the Lamb."

13
The Beloved Physician—Luke

Only Luke is with me (2 Tim. 4:11).

I

The text is a strange mingling of songs and sobs. It laughs out loud with irrepressible gladness. It also sighs with a grief that is soaked in tears. There is sunshine in it, bright as the splendours of cloudless noon. There is also darkness in it akin to that of a night without stars. Here is a bit of spring-time, a-riot with colour and fragrance and tuneful with the song of birds. Here also is bleak winter, colourless and cold, with the bitter winds wailing through the skeleton boughs of the trees.

"Only Luke is with me." Whence the tearfulness of this sentence? Why is it grief-filled as the heart of a mother who has lost her first-born? For this reason it tells of absent ones whom the apostle misses and for whose presence he deeply longs. Some of these are away on errands of service; they are away on missions upon which he has sent them. He misses them, and yet there is joy in their very absence. They are at the post of duty. But there is one whom he misses who is not at the post of duty. Yesterday he was here. Today he is away. And the apostle cannot keep back his tears as he writes, "Demas hath forsaken me, having loved this present world." "Only Luke is with me."

But while the old hero weeps as he writes this sentence, his tears flow over a face that is still bright with an inner joy. For even though Demas has gone, even if the love of the world has gripped him, even if in this Vanity Fair called Rome, he has forgotten his high quest and has deserted his old friend, there is still one who is faithful and true. If Demas has proved unreliable, if he has turned his back upon friend and duty and God, there is one who still stands by with unshaken loyalty. There is one who remains steadfast. There is one upon whose fidelity he can count with absolute confidence. The crowd may pass him by in utter forgetfulness, his friends may be ashamed of his chain, but there is one who will never be ashamed. And so, with inner laughter, he writes, "Luke is with me."

II

Who is Luke?

Who is this man upon whom Paul counts with such absolute assurance? Is he one who is bound to the Apostle by close ties of flesh and blood? No, Luke and Paul are no kin. Are they brought together by the bonds of a common nationality? No, Paul is a Jew and Luke is a Gentile. A few years ago they were separated by the very widest of chasms. And yet we find them here bound together by the closest bonds of friendship and of brotherhood. They are brothers because they are worshippers of a common Lord. They have experienced the redeeming love of a common Saviour. They who yesterday were afar off both from each other and from God have been brought near by the blood of Christ.

When did Luke become a Christian? We do not know. How was he converted? Here again we must answer that we do not know. But of this we can speak with absolute assurance. Luke is converted now. That man watching outside Paul's prison cell has a present experience of the saving grace of Jesus Christ. And, mark you, that is the important matter. A very earnest man said to me not long ago that he would not give the snap of his finger for the Christianity of any man who could not tell the day and the hour in which he was converted. It is good to know when you were converted, but it is not necessary. There is something far more important than that. It is this: to know that you are converted now. You may have a very clear memory of how Jesus Christ came into your life a quarter of a century ago, but that is of no avail unless He has a place in your heart today. It is well to be able to sing "At the Cross where I first saw the light." But it is far better to be able to sing "Blessed Assurance, Jesus is Mine."

Some of you good mothers have been married almost half a century. Suppose when you get home today your husband should tell you how beautiful you were years ago when he led you a blushing bride across the threshold of his home. Suppose he were to grow enthusiastic about how charming you looked before you had divided the roses upon your cheek with daughters that are now mothers, and before you had given your strength to sons that are now fathers. There would be little thrill in all that unless he should pass on to tell you of his feelings toward you now. You would want to hear him say: "Though 'the last feather of the raven's wing has fallen from your hair,' and though there are more wrinkles on your face than there are graves in the cemetery over which we have wept together, still you are more beautiful and far dearer than you were on that distant day when love's morning had its dawn."

And it is the present tense of your Christian experience that is of supreme value. How you were converted, when you were converted, where you were converted, all these questions are interesting, but they are not essential. The only big question is, "Do you know Jesus now?" Can you look into His face this moment and say, "My Lord and my God"? If you can do that, you need never worry yourself about dates. If you can do that, you need never worry yourself about the findings of the critics. A young fellow from our Southland came home from the war to find a big writeup of himself in the paper, telling how and when he was killed at the battle-front. The article was well written and sounded altogether truthful. But the living soldier did not accept the statement of the paper, even though the article was written by one who was evidently both cultured and honest. We know that Luke was a Christian because we see him living the life.

III

Another fact that we know about him is that he was a physician. No doubt he was a practising physician before he was ever converted to Christianity. When Jesus got hold of him He did not call upon him to throw away his old profession and take up one that was altogether new. He called him to the doing of his old task under new motives and in the energy of a new power. It is true that Dr. Luke performed other services that are not peculiar to the medical profession. But it was as a physician that he performed these services. A physician he was at the time of his conversion and a physician he remained to the end of the day.

And Luke's case is not peculiar. The call of God to most of us is not into new fields of service. Of course for some to yield to God is to be called into the ministry. For others to yield is to be called into the foreign field. But for most of us to put ourselves into Christ's hands is to toil at our same task, to work in the way in which we have been working, but to do that in the inspiration of a new power and in the joy of a new fellowship. Dorcas does not throw away her needle when she becomes a Christian. She simply consecrates it to Christ. Luke does not throw away his bandages and his healing medicines. He uses them to the glory of God. The business man does not quit his business. He conducts it as a good steward of Jesus Christ.

God does not want all of us to do the same thing. We cannot all render the same service. But we can all render some service. Dr. Luke cannot preach like Paul, neither can Paul heal like Luke. This kind physician has a task all his own. And it would be hard to find one that is capable of being used more to the glory of God. The physician who goes to his work as God's man carries something to his patients that is better than his skill, however skillful he may be. Blessed the patient that falls into the hands of a physician whose powers have been dedicated to his Lord. There is no end to the service that is rendered by such a man. He is a fellow worker with the Great Physician.

IV

But Dr. Luke did more than practise medicine. He was a writer of great brilliancy and power. Thus he has brought the whole world into his debt. There are sixty-six books in the Bible. Sixty-four of them were written by Jews. Only two of them were written by a Gentile, and the Gentile that wrote these two was Dr. Luke, the Christian Physician. And these two books are about as choice bits of literature as even the Word of God contains. It is to Luke we are indebted for the thrilling story of the conquest of the early Church. It is he that tells of the coming of the Promise of the Father on the day of Pentecost. It is Luke who tells us of Peter's inspired sermon on that day, and of the conversion of the three thousand. It is Luke who lets us into the intimate fellowship of the great saints of that day—Paul, Peter, Barnabas, and others.

Then we are indebted to Luke for the third Gospel. Renan called this Gospel of Luke the most beautiful book ever written. It tells of course the same story as that told by the other evangelists, and yet there are touches that make it far different. Luke was not writing to the Jews, but to the Gentiles. He was writing especially for ourselves. Naturally he does not place his emphasis always where the other evangelists place theirs. He goes beyond them, as others have pointed out, in giving emphasis to at least two important truths.

A. It is Luke who emphasises the universality of Christ's forgiving love. Matthew makes the wise men ask, "Where is He that is born King of the Jews?" Matthew has the Jews in his eye as he writes. But when Luke writes the story he gives no prominence to the Jewish claim. "And lo, the Angel of the Lord came upon them, and the glory of the Lord shone round about them; and they were sore afraid. And the Angel said unto them, Fear not: for, behold, I bring you good tidings of great joy, which shall be to all people. For unto you is born this day in the city of David a Saviour, which is Christ the Lord." Then Luke proceeds to tell us story after story in which he emphasises the fact that his good tidings are really meant for all the people.

Down in the rich city of Jericho there was a man named Zaccheus. This man was a publican. He had sold himself to a foreign power. He wore the livery of Rome, and, therefore, he was more despised than if he had worn the garb of a slave. This man was rich, but he was an outcast. He was rich, but he was hated and shunned, and every door to decency was shut in his face. But one day Jesus Christ came that way and invited Himself to be a guest in the home of this despised grafter. And Jesus Christ said to him: "Today is salvation come to thy house." Luke is the only one that tells us this story.

Then one night there is a feast in the house of a certain Pharisee. Jesus is a guest. During the meal there is a disturbance. A berouged woman of the street steals in from out the dark. She falls down at the feet of Jesus and washes them with her tears.

Then she undoes the cascade of her hair and wipes those feet with the hairs of her head. And Simon, the Pharisee, shudders with horror because the Master allows Himself to be touched by this soiled rag of womanhood. But Jesus declares that her sins that are many are forgiven because she loves much. We owe that precious bit to Luke.

But the finest story ever written has not yet been mentioned. It begins like this: "A certain man had two sons, and the younger of them said to his father, Give me the portion of goods that falleth to me. And he divided unto them his living. And not many days after the younger son gathered all together and took his journey into a far country, and there wasted his substance in riotous living." It is needless to tell the whole story. It is about the most familiar in the literature of the world. And the reason it is so familiar is because, above all other stories, it reveals the compassionate and tender heart of our Heavenly Father. It tells us how eternally eager He is to give heaven's best even to those who have wasted their substance in riotous living. Luke makes most plain to us the universality of the forgiving love of God.

B. It is Luke also who emphasises the perils of prosperity. Come all you who would be rich and read and re-read the Gospel of Luke. Do you remember that story that Jesus told of the rich farmer? Do you recall the man who was so pressed by the work of barn building that he had no time for soul building? Do you recall him who was so busy piling up treasure for the few days in which he might live that he utterly forgot to make any provision for the eternity in which he must live? Do you recall that shrewd man who one day tumbled into his abundant crops and got drowned just as you have seen a bee get drowned in its own honey? Did you ever sit down and let the Rich Fool tell you what a perilous something is prosperity? It is Luke who has preserved for us this startling story.

It is Luke also who tells us of another very prosperous man called Dives. No charge is made against this man. He is simply shown to us for a typical day in his life. He is dressing well and trying to get rid of some of his money by giving banquets. There is a beggar at his gate, but he does not see him. He is too busy trying to amuse himself. Therefore, he neither helps this beggar nor does he drive him away. He simply lets him alone. Then one day death comes for this rich man, and he leaves his palace dreaming of the bosom of Abraham only to hang his daintily sandalled foot in the rags of the old beggar at his gate and fall flat into hell. Truly Luke forces us to see how right was the Master when He said, "How hardly shall they that have riches enter into the Kingdom of God."

V

What kind of a man was Luke?

A. We would like much to know. But Luke was not good at having his picture made. He took absolutely no pains to leave us a life-size picture of himself. In fact he kept his own face hidden as much as possible. But he revealed this much in spite of himself: that he was a scholar. Luke was one of the best trained men of his time. He was a man of wide reading and accurate information. He was capable of mental fellowship with St. Paul, and St. Paul was one of the intellectual giants of all time. It is true that Luke does not tell us what university he attended, nor what degrees he had. He is too modest for that. But no thoughtful man can read his books without realising that he is reading from a painstaking and well-trained scholar.

B. Another fact that Luke cannot conceal about himself is his beautiful modesty. He lets us into the secret not by what he says, but by what he fails to say. When he wrote his Gospel, for instance, it was necessary for him to interview many notable people. The Virgin Mother was doubtless among these. But he does not tell us so. In fact he never mentions his own name in all the story. And when he wrote The Acts, though he himself was a part of some of the stirring stories that he tells, yet here again his name is never mentioned. There is no use to ask Luke's left hand what his right hand is doing. You will not get the least information. He sees to it that such matters are kept secret. How beautifully Christ-like he is in his modesty! He does the work, but he does not see fit to tell us who did it. He paints the picture, but he does not put his own name in the corner when the job is finished. He presents us with two of the most beautiful and helpful books ever written. But when we look over on the flyleaf we see that he forgot to autograph them. When we turn the pages, though we look carefully, we fail to find any calling card. A modest and scholarly man was Luke.

C. Luke was lovable. Paul calls him the Beloved Physician.

And is it not a great privilege to be loved? Why is it that we love some folks? Answer: Some folks are so lovable. There are some people that we cannot resist. We may hear things about them that we do not like. We may come to them with pre-conceived notions and with unfair prejudices, but their presence strikes the death blow to all these enemies of love. Our hearts capitulate and we yield to them in spite of ourselves. Luke was like that. He took the heart of Paul captive, and the heart of many another. What ammunition did he use? Can you not guess? He used love. There is no conqueror of hearts like that. It is the weapon that God Himself uses for the conquest of you and me. "We love because He first loved us." If you want to be lovable—and that is a prize to be coveted—if you want to be as attractive as a garden caressed by the springtime, if you want to be as sweet and winsome as the music of the mocking bird, then let love into your life. Folks can resist logic; they can resist the best arguments, but they melt like snow at the sun's kiss under the mighty influence of love.

D. Luke was steadfast. He was modest and loving and lovable, but that did not keep him from having the heart of a lion. The touch of his hand was as soft as the touch of a mother, but he was not soft in his moral fibre. He was a man of the hardiest courage. It is a tremendous help in fighting a hard fight to have the companionship of comrades. It is exceedingly encouraging when we are facing danger to know that brave hearts are standing by our side. Luke needed this encouragement, but it was not absolutely essential. "Dr. Luke, Paul has lost his popularity. The crowds have turned from him." "Then," said Luke, "I will do without the crowds. By the grace of God I am able to stand alone."

And Paul, with an appreciation that sets his burdened heart to singing, takes his pen and writes, "Only Luke is with me." What a fine virtue is that of steadfastness. How God needs men and women in the Church that can be relied upon. Every church has a few of this kind. The pastor soon learns them. When the prayer meeting comes, they are there. When the revival comes, they are there. When the day is ugly and stormy and few find their way to God's house, they are among them. They are dependable. They are steadfast. They are those to whom God will be able to say by and by: "You have been faithful." When I see Luke watching alone outside the prison cell of Paul, my heart fairly bows the knee within me in honour of him. Thank God for Luke.

"Only Luke is with me." And the man who writes this pathetic sentence is in disgrace and in prison. But Luke does not choose his friends because of their popularity nor because of their success in the eyes of the world. He may be counted on in the days of prosperity. He may be counted on no less in the days of adversity. A great, brave, loyal soul is he. He is modest, lovable, steadfast. Thus Paul could write of him, "Only Luke is with me." And it is my conviction that if Paul were writing a letter to us today from "Life's Other Side," he could say this same word, "Luke is with me." Luke was with him in the battle, he stood by him in death, and these friends have found each other about the Round Table of the King. May God give us something of the winsomeness and the steadfastness of Luke, the Beloved Physician.

14

The Quest for the Best

The kingdom of heaven is like unto a merchant man, seeking goodly pearls: who, when he had found one pearl of great price, went and sold all he had, and bought it (Matt. 13:45, 46).

It is evident that Jesus regards this merchant with whole-hearted approval. He admires his energy, his purposefulness, his clear-eyed good sense. He is fairly fascinated by his decision of character, and by the sanity and courage that lie behind it. "Here is one," he seems to say, "that is possessed of a knowledge that is most worth possessing. He knows how to use life." And surely his is a knowledge that is all too rare. There is a story of a man who owned a fine old violin. But instead of learning to make vocal the angel choir that homed within it, he used it merely as a prop to keep open the door of his cabin. Thus often we, too, foolishly fumble the big business of living. That we may avoid such tragedy, let us give earnest attention to this wise merchant. There are four facts about him that are well worthy both of our consideration and imitation.

I

First, he is possessed of a definite purpose. He has come to terms with himself. He knows exactly at what mark he is going to aim and what goal he is going to seek. Of course the advantages of this are many. To mention one, it is a primary essential for joyous living. No purposeless soul is ever happy. Life never becomes truly songful till it is tuned and touched by the skilled fingers of a worthy purpose. Much of the prevailing restlessness and wretchedness of our day is born of sheer aimlessness. Too many are possessed by the joyrider's attitude toward life. They are indifferent both as to direction and destination. They have as much business at one place as at another. Thus they not only burn up their energies without getting anywhere, but they even miss the joy of the ride. That bright young chap that flung out of life the other day by suicide did so to escape the intolerable boredom of purposeless living. But this man has a real reason for carrying on. Therefore we may congratulate him for he is headed for the sunrise.

Then purpose makes for power. It is said there is heat enough in an acre of sunshine to blast the very rocks like bits of gunpowder if the rays were only focalized. There are also energies enough in the weakest of us for the accomplishment of worthwhile tasks if these energies are only focalized. That which is needed to focalize them is a dominant purpose. When we read that Daniel purposed in his heart, we know at once that Babylon must reckon with him. It can no more ignore Daniel than it can ignore the law of gravitation. He became a power. He is one still. The centuries have dealt harshly with the big city that once stood upon the Euphrates. They have torn down its high walls, desecrated its palaces and temples, and kicked its swinging gardens into heaps of rubbish. In fact, nothing is left of the Babylon of that distant day but the character of Daniel. His purpose made him stronger than the passing years. We, therefore, congratulate this purposeful merchant because he is on the pathway to strong and gladsome living.

II

The second fact that challenges our admiration about this man is that he not only has a good purpose, but he has the highest possible. He is not simply a seeker after the good; he is a seeker after the best. He is out upon a quest for pearls. He is something more than a mere merchant, a maker of money. He is a connoisseur of pearls. Now the pearl was the most priceless jewel in that day. In seeking for pearls, therefore, he was seeking for those values that are supreme. And on such a high quest should you and I be bound. For the very best is within reach of all our hands if we are but willing to pay the price. And because we can claim the best, it becomes our solemn duty to do so. No one of us has a right to be satisfied with any lesser values than those that are supreme.

But how far beneath our privileges do many of us fall! There are some that make choice of that which is worthless. There are even those that choose what is worse than worthless, the positively vicious. But it is not the quest of the vicious that I fear for most of you, it is rather the quest of the trifling, or the quest of the second best. The question of right and wrong is not so compelling today as it should be. There has been a breaking down of old sanctions, a flinging away from old standards and restraints. The difference between right and wrong is to many as vague and hazy as the horizon on a misty morning. Suppose then we bring this test. Are the ends we are seeking worthwhile? Are they important or are they trivial? Are they of supreme value or are they merely secondary?

This story is told of a certain well-known gentleman who was somewhat given to dissipation. He went one day to Johns Hopkins Hospital for a medical examination. When his physician had looked him over carefully, he said, "Mr. A, if you give up coffee and tobacco, and above all else, quit drinking liquor, you may live for ten years." And the patient answered in the tone of bewilderment, "What for?" That is, life for him consisted in eating and drinking. He had no higher aim than the satisfaction of his appetite. Here is another whose purpose is no higher. In fact, I am not at all sure that it is not far lower. He is a keen young business man. He has made up his mind that he is going to be rich. He is going to be worth at least a million dollars. To attain this end, he "scorns delights and lives laborious days." "Why do you wish to be a millionaire?" a friend asks him one day. "So I can tell the other fellow to go to the devil," was his answer. And when we hear that, we fairly blush for the meanness of his quest.

But how about you? What are you after? If you win the prize for which you are now spending your life, what will you have? If you gain the goal toward which you are now driving, where will you park when the sundown comes? You have only one life to invest. What are you buying with it? Some years ago a group of boys were standing on the bank of the Tennessee River when it was at flood. About a hundred yards from the shore there was a lumber stack whose top was just above the water. Suddenly these boys saw a rabbit, that had been driven out of its burrow by the high water, take refuge on that stack of lumber. It was easy to see that the rabbit was too spent to go any further. "I am going out and catch that rabbit," said one of the boys. So he got into a frail canoe, made his way to the lumber stack, caught it, and killed it, and put it down in the pocket of his overalls. He then started back to the shore. But he struck a treacherous current, lost control of his boat, allowed it to capsize, and was drowned. Three days later they found his body. They brought it to land and laid it on the fresh green grass. Then one of his companions came forward and drew the dead rabbit from his pocket and, holding it up, said, "This is the thing for which he gave his life." How cheaply he sold out! Yet many a man who has passed for a success in the eyes of the world has sold out for less.

> I bargained with life for a penny
>   And life would give no more,
> However I begged at evening
>   When I counted my scanty score.
>
> For life is a just employer,
>   She gives us what we ask;
> But once we have set the wages
>   Then we must bear the task.
>
> I worked for a menial's hire,
>   Only to learn dismayed,
> That whatever I had asked of life.
>   Life would have gladly paid.

III

Third, this wise man recognized the best when he found it. He was a judge of values. How important that is! The man who would succeed in any business must be a judge of the values with which he has to deal. If he is not, financial disaster is practically certain. Having grown up on the farm, I once had an idea that I was a fairly good judge of horses. But I made a few trades out in the West during the early days of my ministry that convinced me that my education in this direction was far from complete. Then a few investments in other enterprises have left me with little doubt that Wall Street did not lose much when I entered the ministry. My biggest hope now is to succeed in being an exception to that well-known rule, "Once a sucker, always a sucker." But this merchant knew his business. He could tell the worthful from the worthless. He could tell pearls from paste. He could tell the best from the second best. Therefore, when he found the best, he knew it.

But many of us are not so wise. Again and again we see men turn from values that are real to pursue mere gaudy nothings. No wonder Isaiah shouts after such with frantic earnestness, "Wherefore do you spend money for that which is not bread?" No wonder Paul, in praying for his friends, asks that they may have the wisdom to approve the things that are excellent. What blunders we make! Often we are deceived by outward appearances. We allow mere glamor to bewitch us. Personally, I have never found it in my heart to laugh at the Prince of Morocco. I have been guilty of the same pathetic blunder that he made too often myself. It was very natural for him to believe that the picture of the lovely Portia was in the golden casket. It was so much more beautiful than the casket of base lead or even the one of silver. Was it not reasonable that the beautiful likeness and the beautiful casket should go together? He chose by outward appearances and found not the woman of his dreams, but an ugly death's-head. Thus he learned as many another, that all that glisters is not gold.

Then we are confused by the crowd. We see the multitude madly scrambling after certain things, and we decide that because so many are seeking to win these prizes that they must of necessity be of great value. As a boy, I used to feed the pigs. I would pour out a basket of corn that was ample for all. But often one foolish pig would greedily grab an ear and set out running as desperately as if he had cornered the corn crop of the whole world. But instead of ignoring this foolish fellow, two or three other pigs would set out after him, leaving scores of ears just as good lying on the ground. What was the matter? They simply could not throw off the conviction that, the fact that this companion of theirs who was running so frantically, was proof positive that he had something bigger and better than anything to be had elsewhere. And we, too, are constantly being taken in by this pig-philosophy. How many of us are venturing our very lives in the pursuit of prizes of whose worthfulness we have no better proof than that they are being sought by the crowd.

But what the multitude is seeking is a rather poor test of what is of real worth. There are tests, however, upon which we may rely. Take this, for instance: values that are real meet our deepest needs. They satisfy. This at once rules out mere things. No man, however successful, can ever hope to satisfy the hungers of his heart by his worldly winnings. The soul of the rich farmer was just as restless and starved when his barns were full as it was when they were empty. When Sir Titus Salt was an old man, rich in honors and rich in goods, he stood in his garden one day and watched a snail slowly climb to the top of a little stick. When this slow-moving creature had reached the top, he paused for a moment, then turned and began his descent. And as Sir Titus looked on, he said, "I am like that." And as we listen to him, we marvel how one can possess so much, and yet, of real wealth have so little.

Then real values abide. They are not subject to fluctuations of the stock market. Your bonds are not worth as much today as they once were. The value of your bank stock has declined. It is the same with your real estate. But there are values, thank God, that are still at par. "Now abideth faith, hope, love," and these are as priceless as they were in the most prosperous days that our world has ever seen. Faith is worth just as much in these gray days of depression as it was in the long ago, when it steadied the prophet and enabled him to sing: "Although the fig tree shall not blossom, neither shall the fruit be in the vines; the labour of the olive shall fail, and the fields shall yield no meat; the flock shall be cut off from the fold, and there shall be no herd in the stalls. Yet I will rejoice in the Lord, I will joy in the God of my salvation." Hope is still at par. "My the God of all hope fill you with all joy and peace in believing that ye may abound in hope through the power of the Holy Spirit!" That prayer is as well worth praying today as when it was breathed from the hot heart of St. Paul long centuries ago. Then, of course, love is at par. It is just as priceless now as when it sent Jesus to take little children into his arms or to go out as the Good Shepherd in quest of the sheep that was lost. So precious is it that the richest is a bankrupt without it, while the poor who possess it are infinitely rich. May God grant us an eye for the values that are real! This merchant was not to be confused either by outward appearances or by the crowd. Therefore, when he found the priceless pearl, he knew it for what it was. To his keen eye it dimmed all other pearls as the sunrise dims the stars. At once he knew that his long quest was ended.

IV

The final fact we notice about this merchant is that, having found the pearl, he bought it. This marks the very climax of his wisdom. All his seeking, all his finding, all his keen appreciation of values would have gone for nothing but for this. And it is just here that so many who really seek fail of final victory. Right here may be found the reason for the failure of a vast multitude. How many we meet who are frankly disappointed in their religious lives! They are weak when they might be strong. They are joyless when they might be rejoicing with joy unspeakable and full of glory. They are all but useless when they might be rich in helpfulness. How do we account for these moral dwarfs, these spiritual misfits? They had failed to take the final step and claim the pearl.

Some, instead of buying, try to content themselves by talking about the beauty of the pearl and piously wishing that it was theirs. An old saint stood up in a little prayer meeting on one occasion to give his testimony. His was one of those marvelously beautiful stories, such as we may be sure God writes down in his book of remembrances. There was a note of reality in his voice. The listener heard in it authentic messages from the unseen. When the old gentleman had taken his seat, a young fellow arose and said glibly, "I would give the world for that man's experience." "That is just what it cost me," said the old saint quietly. That is just the price that too many refuse to pay. This priceless pearl is not for the man who merely wishes for it. It is for him who, regardless of cost, wills to possess it.

Then there are those who, finding the price of the pearl greater than they are willing to pay, seek to persuade themselves that it is not so wonderful after all. Aesop's fox is not the only creature that ever found sour grapes. That is a discovery all too common. Take the Ten Spies, for instance. When they went into the Land of Promise and saw the giants, they made up their minds that they did not have the gallantry to possess the land.

Therefore, instead of acknowledging the worthfulness of the enterprise and confessing their lack of grit to see it through, they brought up an evil report of the land. That, I fear, is all too common. Many a young chap is laughing today at his youthful ideas, not because they are so ridiculous, but because he lacks the courage to make them realities. How many are neglecting and all but scorning the program of Jesus, not because they have found a better, but because they lack the grit to follow in his steps! Lacking the courage to possess the pearl, we criticize it and make of our criticism a smoke screen behind which to hid our cowardice.

> Upon a rock stands prone my soul,
>   a diver lean, undressed,
> And looks and fears the shock,
>   and turns and hides its shame in some poor, sorry jest.

There are others still who do not buy because they are waiting for the price to be marked down. They admire the pearl genuinely. They feel sure that one day they are going to claim it. But they are going to wait until it is cheaper. Some years ago I was preaching to the students of one of our oldest colleges. At the close of a service a charming young lady came forward and, taking my hand, said, "I am going to be a Christian." And as I began to congratulate her, she drew back and said: "Oh, I did not mean right now. There are a few things that I don't think a Christian ought to do that I am not ready to give up just yet." She, as many another, was waiting for a kind of "dollar day" in the Kingdom of God. She was hoping to find the pearl of great price among the fingered wares of the bargain counter. Of course she was doomed to disappointment.

But this merchant was not so foolish. When he saw the pearl, his eyes sparkled. "What's the price?" he asks in a voice that he finds it hard to control. And the answer does not frighten him as it has many a less valiant and determined soul. "I will take it," he answers firmly and without hesitation. He then hurries away to change the pearls that he already possesses into gold. What does it matter that these pearls have been his pride! What does it matter that they represent the toil of a lifetime! When he finds a buyer, he pushes them across the counter with eager hands as if they were so much rubbish. He then seizes the gold and hurries with hot haste to the owner of the pearl. There is not a moment to be lost. Suppose another should claim the treasure. He feels that should such be the case, life would not be worth living. And when he counts the price and the pearl is his, his pockets are as empty as the pockets of a shroud, for the pearl has cost him all that he had. But as he goes away with his treasure in his hand there is never a backward look of regret. But the joy that looks out from his eyes tells of the fadeless springtime that has burst on the morning hills of his heart.

Is the story of this wise merchant your story? Have you bought the Pearl? I know you are decent and respectable. I know you belong to the Church. I know that you teach a Sunday-school class. But the question I must press upon your heart is this—have you bought the Pearl? Can you sing out of your own experience, "Blessed assurance, Jesus is mine"? Have you ever taken your place beside Thomas to fall at the feet of your risen Christ and say, "My Lord and my God"? Can you join with Paul in this bracing certainty, "I know whom I have believed, and am persuaded that he is able to keep that which I have committed unto him against that day"? If not, the reason is not far to seek. You have not been willing to pay the price. What is Christ asking from you and me? Not for our money, primarily; not for our work; not for our prayers; not for our tears. He is asking for our unconditional surrender. When we give all, he gives all, and we find the Pearl in no other way.

> Here, Lord, I give myself away;
> 'Tis all that I can do.

15
Perpetual Thanksgiving—Paul

In everything give thanks (1 Thess. 5:18).

This exhortation sent by Paul to a group of his fellow Christians has a decided flavor of the impossible about it. The heights to which it calls seem far too rugged and steep for our feeble feet. So much is this the case that vast numbers of us never think of taking his great word seriously. We simply pass it by, confessing, of course, the reality of the pot of gold, but never forgetting that this gold is at the end of the rainbow, and is therefore quite beyond our reach.

But the Apostle himself was perfectly serious and genuinely sincere in the giving of this exhortation. He believed that it was possible to make every day a Thanksgiving Day. Nor did he hold this high conviction simply as a theory. It was his experience. As you study his life you find him in many a trying situation. At times you find him without his cloak, at times without his books and his parchments. You even find him without his freedom and without his friends. But never once do you find him without his song of thanksgiving.

"In everything give thanks." This is something more than a piece of good advice. Excellent advice it is, but it is far more. It is a command. It is a command that is binding. It brings in its hands the sanction of an infinite authority. "In everything give thanks."

So we see then that gratitude is not a matter that is purely optional. You cannot be a Christian and be grateful or ungrateful just as it suits you. To refuse to be thankful is to refuse to be obedient. And to refuse to be obedient is to refuse to be a Christian at all. So it is only stating a sober truth when we say that it is impossible for a thankless man to be a follower of Jesus Christ.

And you will notice the wide scope of this command. "In everything give thanks." That takes in a sweep so wide, I repeat, that it looks utterly impossible. In fact, it is impossible except we receive help from above. God is constantly calling upon us to do the impossible. It was impossible for the paralyzed man to rise and walk, but as he was willing Christ made the impossible to become the possible. And so God will do in this instance if we will allow Him.

"In everything give thanks." I wonder if we have ever been really serious and in earnest with this command. Notice what it says: "In everything." In the joy things and in the sorrow things, in the laughter-laden things and in the tearful things, in the things bright with morning and the things dark with night. "In everything give thanks."

Now that means that we are to be thankful when we succeed. That we are to be grateful in the moments of prosperity and of victory. It means also that we are to be thankful when we fail. That in the midst of our defeat and our humiliation our hearts are to still be overflowing with gratitude. We are to be thankful when these bodies of ours are athrill with vigor and life. We are also to be thankful when the destroying hand of disease is upon us and we feel ourselves slipping inch by inch into the grave.

"In everything." Truly it is a broad command. We are to be grateful when friends are kind, when they throw bouquets at us, when they grip our hands and tell us how much they appreciate us. We are to be thankful when friends seem unkind, when they throw mud at us instead of flowers, when they pass us by in forgetfulness and cold neglect. We are to be thankful beside the cradle afrolic with life. We are also to be thankful beside the grave gloomy with death.

This is indeed a high standard that our Lord sets for us through His inspired Apostle. But it is a possible standard. He never calls us to do that which through His grace we cannot do. How can we reach that fine mountain height where we will really be able to "In everything give thanks"? How did Paul reach it? He did not do so by getting into circumstances that were altogether favorable. Nor will we. There will never come a time in our lives when everything will come to us right-side up. We are going to have to pass through sorrows and losses, struggles and perplexities. However dry our cheeks are today, one day they are going to be wet with tears. So if we never expect to be thankful in everything until everything gets to be entirely to our liking, then we will never fulfill this command at all. But this gratitude is not a child of circumstances. The truth of the matter is that gratitude is never born purely of our circumstances.

For instance, the most grateful people are not the people who have the most. They are not the people who are blessed with good health and with sound minds and with beautiful homes and with high social circles. The most grateful people that I have met are often the ones who, so far as the world could see, had the least. Read the letters of Paul. He was always breaking out into the gladdest praise. His letters are exultant with thanksgiving. They ring with triumphant hallelujahs. This is true not because Paul had everything. He was being shipwrecked, stoned, hounded, whipped, imprisoned. At last they killed him, but they never killed his gratitude.

How then, I repeat, is this amazing possibility to be realized? Answer, it is to be realized through faith in God. Gratitude is a child of faith. If you ever get to the place where you can really give thanks in everything, you have got to have a very real and very vital grip of God. You have got to believe that Paul speaks the sober truth when he says, "All things work together for good to them that love God." There will be many times, of course, when you do not see how the trials and defeats that come upon you can be for good. There will be many times when you cannot understand. But remember that it is not necessary to understand. It is only necessary to believe.

When Bunyan was shut up in Bedford jail he could not understand just how this could be best. But God wanted him to preach, not simply to the men of his day, but to the men of all time. And so He locked in Bunyan's body that his soul might be out piloting the pilgrims over the eventful road from the City of Destruction to Mt. Zion. Believe me, the rude block of marble must have great faith in the art and in the skill of the sculptor if it is to be grateful while it is undergoing the disturbing strokes of mallet and chisel. But if it can be brought to believe that the sculptor is working toward the liberation of the angel that is pent up within, it can, even for these wounding strokes, give thanks.

Our unbelieving eyes looked out the other day and saw only the black clouds and the pouring rain, the soggy streets and the muddy roads and the water-soaked fields. Faith looked out and thanked God and sang:

> It isn't raining rain to me,
>   It's raining daffodils;
> In every dimpled drop I see
>   Wild flowers upon the hills.
>
> A cloud of gray engulfs the day
>   And overwhelms the town;
> It isn't raining rain to me,
>   It's raining roses down.
>
> It isn't raining rain to me,
>   It's raining clover bloom,
> Where any buccaneering bee
>   Can find a bed and room.
>
> So a health to him who's happy,
>   And a fig to him who frets;
> It isn't raining rain to me,
>   It's raining violets.

But while gratitude is a child of faith it is also a child that we must watch and train and develop. Gratitude, as all other fine graces, must be cultivated. It must be tended and watered and watched over or it will die. "In everything give thanks." Do not think that Paul reached this fine height without a struggle. Do not expect to do so yourself. You are not going to do that easily. You are not going to do it lazily and half asleep. You will never realize that high achievement except by conscious effort.

Now how can we help ourselves in the cultivation of this rare and winsome flower called gratitude? In the first place, if you are going to be thankful in everything you cannot begin to do that by ignoring the daily blessings of life which we are accustomed to call commonplace. And yet that is just what most of us have a great tendency to do.

Some time ago I chanced to meet an old friend who has been a great sufferer from a most dreaded disease. But he was then recovered and in perfect health. His dreary days of depression and long nights of wretchedness had passed. And how happy he was. His very presence refreshed like sea breezes. He was simply bubbling over with gladsome praise and thanksgiving. But when I told an excellent woman about this meeting and the great gratitude of our friend what think you she said? This: "Of course! I would be thankful, too, if I had recovered from that terrible disease." Yet she seemed to forget to thank God that she had never even been sick at all.

Did you ever hear of that morning when the sun did not rise? One day—but it was not day. Six o'clock came and no roses bloomed in that far garden of the East. Seven o'clock came and still no sun and no ray of light. Then eight, then nine, then ten, then noon and at noon it was as black as midnight. At noon no bird sang. There was only the hoot of the owl and the swoop of the bat. The world lay dark and silent and asleep.

Then came the black hours of the black afternoon. And there was no sunset because there was no sunrise. And there was no retiring to bed where the weary sleep the "sleep that knits up the raveled sleave of care." Instead people remained wide awake. Some wept, some wrung their hands in anguish. Every church was thronged to its doors with people upon their knees. Thus they remained the whole night through and then millions of eager and tear-wet faces were turned toward the east. And when the sky began to grow red and the sun looked up once more, there went up a shout of great joy that was fairly echoed from star to star. Now a hundred million lips said, "Bless the Lord, O my soul."

Why were these people so thankful? It is the strangest reason in the world. They were thankful because the sun failed to rise for one whole day. And thus the very constancy of God's blessings sometimes seems to kill our gratitude. We are so like little children. Take your child a toy every day when you go home and it will not be two weeks before he will cease to appreciate it, will even feel himself wronged if it fails in a single instance to come.

Cultivate then the fine habit of being thankful for life's daily blessings. Appreciate God's mercies that are new every morning. Commonplace as they seem they are the blessings without which life would not be worth the living. Appreciate the sunrises and the sunsets, the springtimes and the autumntides, the comforts of home, the handclasp of friends, the confidence of associates, the clinging love of the inner circle. Appreciate the open Bible, the Church with its welcome, the constant invitation to the place of prayer and the wide open gateway into the Father's house.

"In everything give thanks." If we do this we must, in the second place, fling away our pride and self-sufficiency and conceit. Did you ever notice how prone we are to blame others for our misfortune and to thank ourselves for our good fortune? The Rich Fool made a fine crop, but he congratulated nobody but himself. He thanked only his own prudence and keenness and sagacity.

How different was Paul. Having returned from a successful missionary journey he does not relate what he has done, but what God has done through him. Preaching before Agrippa and the great crowd in Cæsarea he does not boast of the wisdom that has enabled him to live in spite of bitter enemies. But he says: "Having therefore obtained help of God I continue unto this day." When accounting for himself this alone is his claim: "By the grace of God I am what I am."

May the Lord teach us a like wisdom. For what have I, what have you that we have not received? Have you ability in any direction? Are you physically attractive? Have you beauty? It is no mean gift. Have you strength of mind and of body? Have you a task, a place to work and skill to fill your place? If so, appreciate it. Remember that you have not simply yourself to thank for it. The truth of the matter is that there is not a single blessing that you possess today for which you have only yourself to thank.

If you have a tendency to self-conceit, ask yourself how much would be left if God took from you everything except what is due to yourself alone. If He should do so, civilization would be gone. You did not make it. This city would vanish. You did not build it. The sun would suddenly go out in the sky; the stars would vanish; this solid earth would drop like an anchor into the sea; the sea would vanish; your body would melt into thin air and your immortal soul would be annihilated. So if there is a single thing you value this morning give thanks for it because it comes to you as a gift.

Then if you are going to be grateful in everything you must, in the third place, refuse to allow the blessings of others to make you despise your own. It is strange that we should be so foolish and so wicked as to do this and yet we often are. Saul appreciated the praise that was given to him till he found that David had greater praise. You appreciated the little daisy that was put into your hand till you saw that a friend of yours had an American Beauty rose. You enjoyed your Ford till your friend began to ride in a Packard. Oh, you will never be grateful in that way.

Now, if you are obliged to contrast, contrast yourself as you are today with what you might have been but for the good and tender mercy of your Lord. Do you remember the demoniac that Jesus healed? He wanted to go with the Master, you remember, but Jesus sent him home. Do you suppose this man thought of John leaning upon the bosom of Jesus and plucked up the flower of gratitude and planted the nettle of envy in its place? No, I rather thank that when he was so tempted he thought of the tombs in which he used to live and of the fetters with which men used to try to bind him and of the demons that once possessed him. And thinking of these things the nightingales of gratitude began to sing in the garden of his heart.

Last of all, if you are going to be thankful in everything you must cultivate the habit of giving expression to your thanks. That is what Paul did. He was forever telling his Lord and telling his friends how thankful he was. Constantly he was giving expression to his gratitude. And the more he gave expression to it the more thankful he became. For we are rich in the fine wealth of gratitude just in proportion as we give it away.

Of course those of us who never praise have a good excuse for our silence. Here it is:—God knows or our friends know that we are grateful. But that is not enough. God desires that we "give thanks." And we in this particular are like our Lord. How many starved hearts there are in the world because we fail to give expression to our gratitude. And how many of us allow our gratitude to become weak and sickly and often utterly dead because we fail to give expression to it.

One time a most wonderful preacher visited a certain village. In that village there were ten men who were dying of a hideous and loathsome disease. These wretched men formed themselves into a committee and asked this preacher for help. And the heart of the preacher was tender and his power great. So he responded to this committee of rottenness by healing them every one. This done, nine of them said: "He knows how grateful I am." And having so said they hurried away and ceased to be grateful at all. The tenth man came and fell down at his Savior's feet, giving Him thanks. And when he arose he had tenfold more gratitude than he had when he came. Therefore I urge, "Let the redeemed of the Lord say so."

Now what is the good of being grateful? "In everything give thanks." Why? The Apostle gives just one big reason. "This is the will of God." That is reason enough, is it not? He said be thankful in everything because God wants you to be. That is the way and the only way to please Him.

Why does our gratitude please God? First, because it is a mark of Christian growth in ourselves. Gratitude is a test of character. No baby is grateful. You can take your little fellow when he has the colic and walk the floor with him for seven long hours, and then when you put him down he will never say "Much obliged." He will just yell a little louder. Now we do not blame him, simply because he is a baby. But to continue to be ungrateful is to always be an infant. If you have no gratitude in your heart this morning that shows in itself that you are a moral dwarf. You may have the body of a giant and the mentality of a Shakespeare but you have the soul of a pigmy.

To be a thankful Christian is pleasing to God, in the next place, because to be grateful is one of the roadways to usefulness. Gratitude makes you helpful. It makes you helpful because it begets gratitude in others. Did you ever turn away from seeing some sick body who had neither health nor money nor social position and yet was full of gratitude? And you said to yourself: "Just look what I have. How thankful I ought to be." And you were helped toward gratitude by the gratitude of another.

Then we are helpful in other ways. How a little gratitude strengthens us sometimes. How much better we work when we know we are appreciated. Oh, I fancy that all the machinery of this world would run with infinitely greater smoothness if we would just oil it now and then with the fine oil of appreciation. We think lovely things. We say lovely things when folks are dead. But the trouble is we so often keep them secret while they are alive.

One day you look over the way and see crêpe on the door of your friend. You hurry over to where he lies asleep and spill a thousand grateful words into an ear that does not hear and into a heart that is not helped. But how much you might have helped if you had been in time. That was the fine thing about Mary. She gave expression to her appreciation and she did it on time. "She came aforetime," said the Master. That is, Mary with love's intuition saw Death coming in the distance, and she said, "I will beat Death to Him." And she did. So when Death touched His forehead it made even his old frozen fingers smell of perfume. This because Mary had been on time in giving expression to her gratitude.

> If I should die tonight,
> My friends would look upon my quiet face
> Before they laid it in its resting-place,
> And deem that death had left it almost fair,
> And laying snow-white flowers upon my hair,
> Would smooth it down with lingering caress—
>   Poor hands, so empty and so cold tonight!
>
> If I should die tonight,
> My friends would call to mind, with loving thought,
> Some kindly deed the icy hand had wrought,
> Some gentle word the frozen lips had said—
> Errands on which the willing feet had sped;
> The memory of my selfishness and pride,
> My hasty words, would all be put aside,
>   And so I should be loved and mourned tonight.
>
> O friends, I pray tonight,
> Keep not your kisses for my dead cold brow.
> The way is lonely; let me feel them now.
> Think gently of me; I am travel-worn,
> My faltering feet are pierced with many a thorn.
> Forgive! O hearts estranged, forgive, I plead!
> When ceaseless bliss is mine I shall not need
>   The tenderness for which I long tonight.

Then gratitude is pleasing to God because God is a lover and love always wants to be appreciated. Understand, love will live without it, but it lives in grief and pain and disappointment. If you love anybody the keenest wound that they can inflict upon you is the wound of ingratitude. The high-water mark of English tragedy is King Lear. And what is the climax of this tragedy? It is the father learning "how sharper than a serpent's tooth it is to have a thankless child."

Did you ever read of how those that feared the Lord spoke about it and how a book of remembrance was kept? I wonder if the recording angel will be able to write your name and mine this morning in the gilded volume of those who are thankful. Believe me, you can bring no greater joy to your Lord than the fulfilling of this command: "In everything give thanks."

16
The Supreme Question—The Philippian Jailer

What must I do to be saved? (Acts 16:30, 31).

That question was asked by a startled jailer. He was amidst strange and perplexing happenings. He had just seen wonderful sights. He was being shaken by unfamiliar terrors. For these terrors he sought relief and so he asked this infinitely wise question: "What must I do to be saved?"

But this jailer is not the only man that has ever asked that question. He is not the first man that asked it. This is a universal question. Men of all times and of all climes have asked and sought an answer to this question. The cultured Greeks tried to answer it by building altars to many gods. Then realizing that they had missed it, they sought further by building an altar to the "the Unknown God." It was in an effort to answer this question that children were once sacrificed to the fire god, Moloch. And it is the struggle to answer the same question that causes the Indian mother today to cast her baby into the Ganges and to come home with empty arms and with an empty heart.

I heard a missionary from the heart of Africa say some years ago that he used to live among the savage tribes of the far interior. They were people of the lowest type. They wore no shred of clothing. But in their wild and barbarous religious dances they would swing round and round till they frothed at the mouth and fell down rigid. It was their way, said the missionary, of asking the supreme question: "What must I do to be saved?"

This was a dramatic moment in this jailer's life. It was a moment big with blessing. Look at the picture. Two strange preachers have come to this Roman city of Philippi. Their preaching has brought them into conflict with the authorities. They are drawn before the magistrates. Their clothing is torn from them and they are severely beaten.

It seems that this would have been shame enough and pain enough, but it was not. They were then turned over to a callous and cruel Roman jailer with the order that he should keep them fast. So he threw them into the inner dungeon and made their feet fast in the stocks. The place was foul and cold and dark. Their backs were lacerated and bleeding. And this was their reward for seeking to bring to men the unsearchable riches of Christ.

Now it was dark enough for these two. But they did not lose heart. First they prayed. I can imagine they prayed secretly and then they prayed aloud. And those people in prison heard the voice of prayer for possibly the first time in their lives. Now, real prayer always makes things different. It brings us a consciousness of God. And so as these men prayed their hearts grew warm and joyous till by and by prayer gives place to praise and they begin to sing.

I have wondered what these people sang that night. It might have been the Twenty-third Psalm. Or they might have sung, "I will bless the Lord at all times. His praise shall continually be in my mouth. My soul shall make her boast in the Lord. The humble shall hear thereof and be glad." Or the Thirty-seventh Psalm would have sounded well in the darkness of that hideous dungeon,—"Fret not thyself because of evil doers, neither be thou envious against the workers of iniquity. For they shall soon be cut down like the grass and wither as the green herb." But I think the most likely of all is the Forty-sixth: "God is our refuge and strength, a very present help in trouble. Therefore will we not fear though the earth be removed and though the mountains be carried into the midst of the sea."

Whatever they sang it was great singing. I think the angels opened the windows when they heard it. I think it made the very heart of our Lord glad. What a surprise it was to those in that gloomy old prison. They had heard the walls ring with groans and shrieks. They had heard bitter oaths in the night, but songs with the lilt of an irrepressible joy in them—they had never heard anything like that before.

Now as the melody rang through the gloomy cells something else happened. The old building seemed to be shaking with the very power of the music. An earthquake was on and God took this petty prison in His hand and shook it as a dicer might shake his dice box, and all its doors were thrown open and the fetters were shaken from the feet of those that were bound. And the old jailer is shaken out of his complacency and out of his bed and a great terror grips him.

I can see him as he picks himself up and looks about him in dismay. The doors are open. He is sure that the prisoners are gone. He knows that his life will be to pay. He will not face the shame of it. He will inflict justice upon himself. He draws his sword and prepares to thrust it through him, but Paul's eyes were upon him, and knowing his purpose he shouts at him, "We are all here, Jailer. Do thyself no harm."

There is love in that cry, tenderness in it, longing in it that the jailer could not understand. Neither could he fail to realize the might of it. It touches him deeply. He is gripped by another terror, the terror that has come through the presence of these strange men who have brought the things of eternity to seem real to him. And urged on by that new terror he rushes to these men of bleeding backs and tattered garments and throws himself at their feet with this great question in his heart and upon his lips, "Sirs, what must I do to be saved?"

Now, I am aware of the fact that this jailer was a heathen and I am not accusing him at all of being a great theologian. I do not know how learned he was. I do not know whether he could read or write or not. I do not know whether he was widely traveled or not. He may have never been beyond the precincts of his own city. But what I do know is this, that he asked the biggest question that ever fell from human lips. There can be no greater. It was the greatest for him. It is the greatest for you. It is the greatest for me. "What must I do to be saved?" There is no question quite so big as that.

And I am wondering now if it is a big question to you. Remember, it is not: What must I do to be decent? It is not: What must I do to be respectable? These things are all right, but they are not supreme. It is not: What must I do to get rich? Millions of us are asking that question as if it were the one question of eternal importance. But you know that it is not. It is not: What must I do to be beautiful? Some of us are asking that question too, and some of us, I am sorry to say, are missing the answer to it very much. But that is not the big question. The supreme question is: "What must I do to be saved?"

What is implied in this question when it is asked intelligently? There is implied, first of all, that there is an absolute difference between being saved and lost. There is implied in it that there are two classes of people, not the cultured and the uncultured, not the learned and the unlearned. They are the saved and the lost. They are those that have life and those that do not have life.

I am perfectly aware that we of today do not like such dogmatic divisions. But I call your attention to the fact that they are the divisions that are made in the New Testament. They are the divisions that Jesus made. He puts folks into two classes, and only two. There were two gates, one was broad and the other narrow. There were two foundations on which a man might build, one was of sand and the other of rock. Mark you, He did not divide men into the perfect and the imperfect, but into those that had life and those that did not have it. And it was He that said, "He that hath the Son hath life, and he that hath not the Son hath not life." So this question, if it means anything, means that there is such a thing as being saved and there is such a thing as being lost. That fact is recognized throughout the entire Bible.

This question implies, in the second place, a consciousness of being lost. "What must I do to be saved?" When this man asked that question there were many things about which he was uncertain. He was uncertain as to how he was to get out of his darkness. He was uncertain as to how he was to be saved, but of one thing he was sure—he was dead sure that he was lost. He did not try to dodge that fact. He did not shut his eyes to it. He did not try in any way to deny it.

And, if you are here without God I hope you will not deny it. For if you have not taken Jesus Christ as your personal Savior you are lost. Then the best thing you can do, the first step to be taken in the direction of getting saved, is to realize your lostness. A man will not send for the physician unless he believes himself sick. He will not try to learn unless he realizes his ignorance.

Neither will he turn to God for salvation unless he realizes that he is lost. Oh, it is a good day for a man when he gets a square look at himself. It is a great day when he has a glimpse of himself as God sees him. It is a great hour when, conscious of his guilt, he bows himself in the presence of Him who alone can save and says, "God, be merciful unto me a sinner."

This question implies, in the third place, not only that the man is lost who asked it, but there that is a possibility of his being saved. "What must I do to be saved?"—and here was a man conscious of being lost, conscious of being sin scarred and stained and guilty, yet he believes, and he is right in believing, that salvation is possible for him. He believes that even he can be saved unto the uttermost. There is such a thing as salvation and it is possible for me, even me, to lay hold of it.

And you too must realize that, otherwise it will do you no good to realize the fact that you are a sinner. It is not enough to know yourself lost. You must also believe that you may be saved. It is not enough to realize that you are weak; you must believe that it is possible for you to be strong. You must believe that even a fluctuating Simon can be made into a rock. You must believe in the power of God to remake men, otherwise for you the question is only a question of black despair.

This question implies, in the fourth place, a willingness to be saved. "What must I do to be saved?" This man is not asking this question to gather material for a future argument. He is no speculator. He is no trifler. He is not even asking it because he is intellectually curious. He is not simply asking that he may know the conditions of salvation. He is asking with the earnest purpose in his heart to meet those conditions.

This question implies, in the fifth place, that while salvation is a possibility for you, you must do something in order to obtain it. "What must I do to be saved?" What sort of answer would you expect to a question like that? What did the apostle say? Did he say, "Do nothing. Let the matter alone. Forget it. Drift?" That is what many of us are doing. No, sir, he said nothing of the kind. He told this man to do something. And this man knew, as you and I know, that if we are ever saved we have got to do something in order to get saved.

I say every one of us knows that, and yet too few of us act as if it were really true. We seem to think that salvation is something that we are going to stumble upon by accident. We seem to think it is something that we are going to receive with absolutely no effort on our part. We act as if we thought it might be slipped into our pockets while we sleep or dropped into our coffins when we die. Ask the question intelligently, heart,—"What must I do to be saved?" Then you will realize that you must do something.

This question implies, in the next place, that the conditions of salvation are not optional; that it is not up to you and it is not up to me to decide just what we will do in order to be saved. You can accept salvation or you can refuse it. You can meet the conditions or you can refuse to meet them. But one thing you cannot do. You cannot decide upon the terms upon which you will surrender. If you are saved at all you must surrender unconditionally.

So the question is, "What *must* I do to be saved?" It is not, What is the expedient thing or what is the respectable thing or what is the popular thing to do in order to find salvation? The conditions are not of your choosing and they are not of mine. God has made them and you and I dare not change them. Therefore, if you are ever saved there is not something simply that you ought to do, but there is something that you absolutely must do.

Last of all, this question implies that salvation is an individual matter. "What must *I* do?" It is not a question of what must God do. He has made full provision for the salvation of the whole world. It is not what must the Church do. It is not what must the preacher do. It is not what must this man that is beside me and this man that is behind me or in front of me do. The question comes to my own heart—"What must *I* do?"

"What must I do to be saved?" You must do something, but there are many things that we are doing that will not save us. If you expect to be saved, in the first place, do not depend on your own goodness. "All your righteousness are but as filthy rags." Do not count on your own decency. No man was ever saved that way. I challenge you to find one single one. I was holding a meeting some years ago and I met a young fellow who told me he was good enough without Jesus Christ. Of course he was not saved. A man who says that virtually tells Christ that He has misunderstood his case altogether and that Calvary was a wasted tragedy so far as he himself is personally concerned.

Neither will you be saved trusting in the other man's badness. I know what some of you are saying to yourselves as I preach. You are telling yourselves one of the oldest lies that was ever told. You are saying, "I would be a Christian but there are so many hypocrites in the Church." How many men give that as a reason, but it is no man's reason. And I never knew one man to be saved by it. Believe me, the shortcomings and the sins of my brother are mighty poor things to depend on for my own personal salvation.

Again, you will not be saved by seeking an easy way. You will never win by catering to your own pride and cowardice. I was conducting a revival in a Texas city some years ago. At the close of one of the services a young lady came forward to shake hands with the preacher. As she did so she said, "I am going to become a Christian." I congratulated her upon her decision, but she answered, "Oh, I do not mean right now. I mean I am going to be very soon."

"You see," she continued, "it is like this: I am going in a few days to visit some of my relatives that live way back in the country. There is going to be a revival nearby. It will be easy for me to make the decision there because nobody knows me. But here it is different. Everybody knows me here and I simply haven't the courage to come out and take an open stand for Jesus Christ." She went into the country as she planned but she was not saved. Of course not. Nobody ever found salvation by catering to his own cowardice and pride and seeking an easy way.

"What must I do to be saved?" There is an answer to this question. It is an answer that is absolutely dependable. There is nothing in all the world of which I am more sure than I am of the correctness of the answer to this question. I am as sure of it as I am of my own existence. I am as sure of it as I am of the fact of God.

I wonder if you are interested to know the answer. Remember that it is the answer to your supreme question. It is the answer to the most important question that was ever asked. It is the most important that you will ever be called to act upon in this world. Does the prospect of an answer quicken your heartbeat? Does it shake you out of your lethargy into intensest interest? It ought to if it does not. For the answer that I give is not the answer of a mere speculator or dreamer. It is the answer of inspiration and it is an answer whose truth has been tested by the personal experience of countless millions. "What must I do to be saved?" Answer: "Believe on the Lord Jesus Christ and thou shalt be saved."

What is it to believe on the Lord Jesus Christ? It is to believe that Jesus Christ can do what He claims to do and what He has promised to do and to depend on Him to do it. Mr. Moody tells us how that he was in his cellar one day when he looked up and saw his little girl making an effort to see him. She could not because it was dark in the cellar. "Jump," said Mr. Moody, "Daddy will catch you." And instantly the little girl jumped. Now, that was faith. That was believing on her father. So the jailer believed on the Lord Jesus Christ. He depended upon Him then and there for salvation.

And what happened? He was saved. That very moment Christ came into the man's heart and he became a new creation. He became possessed of a new joy. He became possessed of a new tenderness.

Did you notice what he did? He took water and washed the stripes of the preachers. Paul and Silas were bleeding when they came to the prison but the jailer did not care. But now that he had found Christ he has already begun to be a partaker of the divine nature. A new love has come to him. He has become tender where he was cruel before. Even so does the power of Jesus Christ make men over.

Now, this question: do you want to be saved? If you do you can be. It is the surest thing in all the world. It is as sure as the fact that night follows day. It is more sure than the fact that if you sow wheat you will reap it, that if you believe on the Lord Jesus Christ you shall be saved. Test the matter now and you will know the blessed fact in your own experience.

17
I'd Avoid Being Half-Baked

Ephraim is a cake not turned (Hos. 7:8).

What is wrong with Ephraim? He is not charged with any crime. He is not accused of being either selfish or cowardly or crooked. The one accusation against him is that he is half-baked. He is like a cake that is well done, even perhaps burned on one side, but entirely raw on the other. Therefore, in spite of the fact that he has good stuff in him, he does not arrive. In spite of the fact that there is no fault to be found with his capacity, he is for all practical purposes useless.

We can see at once that Ephraim is by no means a unique character. We meet men of his kind every day. They are wanting in symmetry. They are not balanced. They are lacking in certain well-roundedness. They have too much of one thing and too little of another. They are creatures who go to extremes. They are often burned to a crisp on one side but utterly raw on the other. They remind us, even as does Ephraim, of a cake not turned.

Some of us are out of balance physically. I had a good friend who served through the first World War. When it was over, before he was mustered out, he was asked to pose for a statue of the typical American soldier. Whether he accepted the invitation or not I do not know. But the reason the invitation was given was that he was so symmetrical. He had an almost perfect body. He did not have lovely eyes and no teeth. He did not have one arm as strong as that of a giant and the other as weak as that of a child.

He did not have one foot of ordinary size and the other big enough to wear one of those seven-league boots. He was chosen because he was symmetrically developed.

Just as we need symmetry of body, we need also symmetry of mind. An unbalanced mind is calamity. When it is too pronounced, it sends its victim to the madhouse. Then we need to keep the balance between the physical and mental. To have a tremendously strong body with a weak mind is not appealing. A hackneyed phrase has crept into our language that describes a certain type of girl. We call her "beautiful but dumb!" Sometimes her beauty of body serves only to accentuate her dumbness, so that her possible charm becomes more of a liability than an asset. The dinosaur had a tremendously strong body, but he lacked a brain to match. He was half-baked. Therefore, the centuries rubbed him out. We need a balanced mind in a balanced body.

Then we need to be symmetrical, not only in body and mind, but also in heart. To have much heart and too little mind is often to be so soft as to do as much harm as good. But to have a keen mind with little heart is merely to be a human icicle. Such may do effective work in many directions, but they have no friends. We may respect them, but we never love them. Often they become a menace to society. The truth of the matter is that the greatest threat to our civilization today grows out of the fact that our hearts have not kept pace with our heads. Therefore, our amazing genius, which should have been used for the making of instruments or the enriching of life, has been too largely used for the making of implements of destruction. Thus, as individuals and as nations, we are half-baked. We, as Ephraim, may be described as a cake not turned.

II

What, then, is the prophet urging? He is urging that individually and socially we should be well-rounded. He is recommending that type of culture which Arnold described as the "harmonious expansion of all our powers." He is urging us to avoid extremes. He is recommending what the ancients called the golden mean. We are to seek to be balanced personalities.

This is what the Latin poet Ovid was teaching in his story of

Daedalus and Icarus. These two, father and son, were exiled on the island of Crete. They sought a way of making their escape. Since they had no ship, their only hope was to fly. The father, being an inventive and practical man, made two pairs of wings. This he did by the use of feathers and wax. When the wings were made, both father and son learned to fly. At last, when they had developed sufficient skill for their adventure, the great day came for their escape. Then the father gave his son final instructions. "Don't fly too low," he urged. "Otherwise enemies from the ground will get you, and you will fail to win your goal. But neither must you fly too high. If you do, the sun will melt the wax and your wings will fall apart, and you will fall with them and thus fail of your purpose." Then he added, "You will go safest in the middle."

Fortified by this word of wisdom, the son set out on his journey. For awhile all went well. Then he began to glory in his newly found powers. Equipped with these wings, he felt able for anything. Therefore, in spite of his father's warning, he climbed higher and higher. Too late he realized that the sun had got in its deadly work. The wax was melted. The wings came apart, and he fell to his death. This was the case not because his adventure was impossible. His father won his way to safety with similar equipment. It was the case not because Icarus refused to make any effort. It was the case because he refused to steer a balanced course. He forgot his father's wise advice that he would go safest in the middle.

What is this poet seeking to teach? He is not merely giving advice to our politicians. No more is he urging us to play the role of the halfhearted or of the colorless neutral. There are those who seek to avoid taking sides on a moral issue at all. Then, even when forced to take sides, these often seek to be neither very good nor very bad. They thus become about the most unattractive and useless individuals in the world. "I hate folks," says the author of Psalm 119, "I hate folks who are half and half." So do we—so does everybody! Such a type was extremely disgusting to Jesus himself. He said, "Because thou art lukewarm, and neither cold nor hot, I will spew thee out of my mouth." This word of the poet is certainly not a warning against desperate earnestness.

What then, I repeat, does Ovid mean? He means that we shall become our best by avoiding extremes, by developing harmoniously. We can understand the good sense of this when we realize the fact that many of our worst vices are only virtues pushed too far. Take economy, for instance. It is wise to conserve our wealth. It is foolish to be reckless and wasteful in the use of money. Money that I have earned represents myself. It is a part of my time. It is a bit of my personality. It is condensed energy. It is pent-up power. It is power that I can release for the helping or the hurting of men. I have no right to be careless in its use. Wastefulness is not only silly; it is wicked. The accusation against the Prodigal Son was that he wasted his substance with riotous living.

The other day I saw a soldier doing his best to give his money away. He was all but forcing it into the hands of strangers. Why was this the case? It was not because he was wise. It was rather because he was drunk. To be indifferent to any kind of value is not sensible. To waste is not wise, but stupid; not big, but little. It is only the small that waste. Big things never do. This is a big world on which we live. But it is not a wasteful world. It has never wasted one single drop of water or one single grain of sand or one single weed or flower. When Jesus fed the multitude, he said, "Gather up the fragments that remain, that nothing be lost." Even our God has nothing to throw away.

But while it is wise and right to be economical, there are those who push their economies too far. There are those who, refusing to make money their servant, allow it to become their master. Beginning by a sane saving, they end in an insane miserliness. Of all the degrading loves that we let into our hearts, there is none more deadly than the love of money. It has a way of blinding our eyes to life's finer values. It has a way of killing our better selves. It has a way of electrogalvanizing us—soul, mind, and body—so that we drop into our coffins at the end of the day with a clank like the ring of a coin. To practice economy is a fine virtue; to push it too far is a most ugly vice.

Then what a beautiful virtue is courage! Of all the virtues, I think it is the most universally admired. It has been admired in all ages. The cave man admired it. The most cultivated of moderns admires it no less. It is admired by the old and by the young, by those in the Occident and by those in the Orient. It is admired by the most learned and by the most ignorant. It is a virtue that is so important that it calls for a grudging respect even in the most unlovely. It is so important that its absence is hard to forgive even in the otherwise lovely.

But as beautiful as courage is, it can be pushed too far. When pushed too far, it becomes recklessness. Now no man has a right to be reckless. Sometimes we claim for certain individuals that they are entirely without fear. Generally speaking, that is not true. It would not be any great compliment if it were. An ordinary bulldog knows little of fear, but he is not for that reason the highest type of hero. When one is so courageous as to be reckless, he endangers his own life as well as that of others. No risk is too great to take for a worthy cause. But to risk the priceless treasure of life for a trifle or for nothing is at once foolish and wicked. Recklessness is only the fine virtue of courage pushed too far.

III

Since we desire to be well rounded, where shall we turn to find one who not only can serve as our model but who can also give us the power for the reaching of our goal? The answer to that question I find in Jesus Christ our Lord. He was the most perfectly balanced, the most beautifully symmetrical character that this world has ever known. If we fail to recognize that, it is because we have never given ourselves a chance really to know him. Let us look, then, at some of the marks of perfect balance and poise that we find in him whom many of us are happy to call our Lord and Master.

A. How tender he was! What a roomy heart he had! There were many outcasts among his people, but not one of them was beyond his interest and love. One day when a group of cruel men threw a soiled rag of womanhood at his feet, demanding that she be stoned, he took her part. He treated her with the same tender courtesy that he would have shown to the purest of the pure. When mothers came into his presence with their babies in their arms, there was always trouble. These little fellows insisted on climbing out of mother's lap and climbing up into the lap of Jesus. It was written of him, "A bruised reed shall he not break and the smoking flax shall he not quench." He was and is the Christ of the battered and bruised and broken folks.

But while he was unspeakably tender, he was never soft. While he was gentle, he was never maudlin. Though his were the kindliest eyes that ever looked upon men, that does not mean that he went about with a smile of approval for every one whom he met. While he commended some with words that thrill us to this day, there were others he rebuked. While he approved some, there were others that he scourged with the sword of his mouth. While there were some for whom he could find no words too tender, there were others for whom he could find no words too bitter. He called them a generation of snakes and wondered in the heat of his moral indignation how they could escape the damnation of hell. He was unspeakably gentle and tender, but he was also unspeakably firm and strong.

B. He was a man of amazing self-control. There are some folks who pride themselves on being high-tempered. They seem to think that it is a mark of strength that they have little self-control. They are as easy to set off as a powder magazine. In a fit of temper they slam doors, kick over chairs, give themselves the luxury of violent language. There was none of that about Jesus. He was tantalized and contradicted as few ever have been. On one occasion without any sufficient provocation a man slapped his face. But Jesus kept his temper and refused to hit back. One of his dearest friends, himself a passionate and fiery man, writing of him forty years after the crucifixion, calls attention to the characteristic in him that I am sure impressed him most. This is what he wrote: "When he was reviled, he reviled not again."

But the fact that Jesus was a man of perfect self-control does not mean that he was a man of ice. A hotter heart than his never beat in a human bosom. At times he fairly blazed with hot anger. One day he went into a church where there was a man with a withered hand. He found that the religious leaders of the day were more concerned in keeping their petty rules than in giving this man help. We read, therefore, that he looked round upon them with anger. It was an anger that scorched and blistered and burned. Those who saw it never forgot it. His was the anger of the "terrible meek." Such anger differs from ours conspicuously in this respect: We usually get angry when we are personally insulted. We can blaze when one interferes with our rights. But Jesus never grew angry over wrongs done to himself but only over wrongs inflicted upon others. It was when weakness was imposed upon by strength, it was when right was outraged by might, that he blazed. It was then that he became fiery-eyed and defiant. Here, then, is a man of hottest passion, but of perfect self-control.

C. Then Jesus was a deeply serious man. He was tremendously in earnest. He was so in earnest that his friends read in his tired face one day the interpretation of a passage of Scripture that they had never understood before. "The zeal of thine house hath eaten me up." He was genuinely in earnest and so deeply serious that he was called "a man of sorrows and acquainted with grief." He was so serious that there were times when his face was wet with tears. There were times that he sobbed as only the brokenhearted sob. Naturally many have come to think of him as one who could never laugh and whose face was seldom if ever lighted by a smile.

But this is very far from telling the whole story. In spite of his seriousness—and because of this fact!— he was the most joyful of men. The artists have done Jesus a great injustice by picturing him as one whose life was one long sob. He did sob, but he also sang. He could laugh. He was possessed of a delicious sense of humor, as any reader of the Gospels can see. In fact, he was so glad that many of his day who looked on religion as a bit of a killjoy did not think that Jesus was religious at all. He was the most earnest of men and yet the most joyful. These two should always go together. The flippant seldom truly laugh, however many laughing noises they make. Those too serious to laugh generally major on minors. Our balanced Christ could both laugh and weep.

D. He was the world's greatest dreamer. One day he locked up his little carpenter shop in Nazareth and went out with no lesser hope than the conquest of the whole world. But while he dreamed he did more. He could "dream and not make dreams his master, and think and not make thoughts his aim." If he was the world's supreme dreamer, he was also the world's supreme realist. Of all the practical men that ever set foot on the planet, he was the most practical. Men and nations must accept his way because life won't work in any other. To turn from him is to face toward chaos and death. In him the idealist and the realist were perfectly blended.

E. He was the most vital of men, with a passionate love of life. It was his abounding vitality that was part of the secret of the spell that he cast over men. Turn the pages of the New

Testament and see how often men came to him to ask him about life. He tells us plainly that he did not lose his life. Instead, he gave it. Superior force did not wrench it from his grudging hands and clinging fingers. "No man taketh it from me, but I lay it down of myself." He was passionately in love with life, but he was glad to die in order to accomplish the will of God.

F. Finally, Jesus was deeply religious. No man was ever more so. But he was never sanctimonious. He never paraded his piety. He never struck an attitude or assumed an unctious tone. In fact, no other man ever hated mere pious talk as he did. Hypocrisy was his pet horror. One day a peddler of pious twaddle broke in on his message with this fine word: "Blessed is he that shall eat bread in the kingdom of God!" But Jesus failed to show the slightest appreciation. Instead, he at once proceeded to tell the story of a "certain man who made a great supper, and bade many: And sent his servant at supper time to say to them that were bidden, Come; for all things are now ready. And they all with one consent began to make excuse." Thus was Jesus reminding this seemingly earnest man that he did not really desire a place at the feast of the fullness of life. He only wished to have a reputation for such a desire. Jesus had the hatred of an intensely sincere man for such pretense. The sanctimonious parader finds nothing but rebuke in his presence.

His hatred of pretense was so intense because his love for reality was so profound. Religion for him meant a deep and clear realization of God. How real God was to him! How constantly he enjoyed his companionship! "He that hath sent me is with me: the Father hath not left me alone; for I do always those things that please him." He was a strong Man, the strongest of the strong; but he never trusted in his own strength. He declared, "I can of mine own self do nothing." He lived his life upheld by a mighty faith in a fatherly God. When he hung on the cross, the worst that his enemies could say of him was, "He trusted in God." The last word that fell from his lips was a prayer that he had learned at his mother's knee: "Father, into thy hands I commend my spirit." He was the most religious of men, yet utterly free of any touch of sanctimoniousness.

Here, then, is One at whose feet we may sit and learn. Here is a well-rounded Man. Here is a Man of perfect symmetry. He offers to be your Friend and mine. Some of you as soldiers and sailors are going out to strange and trying experiences. But you do not have to go alone. Our Christ is eager and able to go with you all of the way. If you give him a chance, he will enable you to feel in the most trying situation that the Eternal God is your dwelling place and that underneath are the everlasting arms. Thus undergirding you, he will also increasingly enable you to possess a poised and balanced personality akin to his own.

18
That Fox—Herod

Go ye, and tell that fox, Behold, I cast out devils, and I do cures today and tomorrow, and the third day I shall be perfected (Luke 13:32).

There is a quiet majesty about that sentence. The Pharisees have come to tell Jesus that he must leave the country because Herod is seeking to kill him. Of course, these Pharisees are not bringing this information because of their friendship to the Master. They are rather seeking to drive him to Jerusalem, where they are going to kill him themselves. But Jesus answers with quiet dignity and assurance, "I am going on about my God-appointed task in spite of what you or Herod may do. I am going to bring this task to completion through my death at Jerusalem." This text throws a strong light on Jesus' consciousness of his mission. It also tells us that his death was not simply a tragic accident, but that it was the very climax of his achievement. It was only through his death that he could utter that tremendous word that he uttered on the cross: "It is finished."

But our present interest in this text is not because of the light that it throws upon Jesus, but upon Herod Antipas. "Go ye, and tell that fox," said Jesus. The Master sometimes rebuked and rebuked very sharply, but he was not accustomed to single out one individual and brand him with any ugly name. But here he calls Herod "that fox." That is startling. No other man ever had so high regard for human personality as did Jesus. He believed in man as man with a faith that nothing could kill. He had a deep reverence for human worth. But here the most reverential and the most loving of all men could find no better name for one of his fellows than "that fox." This word is a window through which we look into the very soul of Herod.

I

What does it tell us about him? What kind of creature is the fox? To us this beast is not greatly repellant. His name does not fill us with horror and make our blood run cold. But the fact that this is the case is not the fault of the fox. The only reason we regard him as a source of amusement in the chase or as a furnisher of fur for ourselves instead of as a dreaded public enemy is because of his physical weakness rather than the possession on his part of any uprightness of character. The fox is a beast of prey. He lives off the bodies of others. He takes without giving. He is cruel, cunning, and heartless. When, therefore, the Master called Herod a fox he was calling him a most ugly name. He was describing a man who at heart was little better than a beast of prey.

Not only is the fox a beast of prey, but he is a little beast of prey. Therefore to his cruelty he adds the contemptible vice of pettiness. He substitutes cunning for courage, speed for strength. Had Jesus called Herod a lion we should have thought of him as cruel and strong, bloodthirsty and courageous. But when he calls him a fox we think of him as at once cruel and cowardly. The fox is only a hero in the hencoop. At the bark of the most cowardly dog he takes to his heels. Thus the picture we get of Herod is that of a shy man who is at once cruel, cowardly, weak, and unprincipled.

The fact that Jesus was right in calling him a fox is indicated by a glance at his life. Take one single episode. One day Herod made up his mind to visit his brother, Philip, who was then residing at Rome. He made the journey and was doubtless received by his brother with all courtesy and respect. But though he was bound to Philip and to Philip's wife by ties of blood, though he owed them the loyalty of a guest, these considerations had no influence at all. He was still the same foxy scoundrel that he ever was. Thus he used the privileges accorded him through this visit to make love to, and to have an affair with, his brother's wife. I suppose he found that Herodias alone understood him. At any rate she consented to elope with him and marry him provided he would send his own wife home. This he consented to do. Thus this fox returned to his palace near the shores of the Dead Sea a bit later, having wrecked both his own home and that of his brother.

Having read this story, we do not wonder that Jesus calls Herod a fox. He was a low, cunning, tricky thief. Of course, you may remind me that Herodias was willing to be stolen. Yet, that fact does not excuse Herod. It is rather strange how often in such matters we decide that an opportunity to play false gives us the right to do so. We do not take the same attitude with regard to lesser values. Take money, for instance. If I were to say to you, "I was down at the bank recently and the cashier left a ten-dollar bill within easy reach of my hand. I seized it at once and slipped it into my pocket. I would consider myself foolish to pass up a chance like that." You would not congratulate me. You would look upon me as a thief. A far greater thief is the man that steals in the moral realm, whatever may be the circumstances. You can see, therefore, the wisdom of the name that Jesus gives to Herod.

II

But while Herod was an evil and corrupt man, he was not altogether evil. That is always the case. No man is ever wholly good, and no man is ever wholly bad. Cunning, cruel, and unprincipled as was Herod, he had a better side to his nature. Among the noxious weeds that grew in the garden of his heart there were still a few flowers. These were sickly and weak and much in need of the sun. But in spite of this they were there making a pathetic effort to grow. Something of this lingering goodness comes out in his relationship to John the Baptist. This great and good man interested Herod immensely, made a tremendous appeal to him, stirred him at times to the depths of his shallow soul.

Just how these two extremes came to meet we cannot say. We are naturally a bit surprised to find foxy Herod occupying a pew in the church of which stern and gallant-hearted John the Baptist is pastor. I can imagine that curiosity played its part in bringing these two together. When John began his ministry in the wilderness he created a great stir. He fairly emptied the villages and cities round about to fill the silent solitudes along the banks of the Jordan with multitudes of eager listeners. He preached a rather stern and harsh gospel, but he did it with such fiery conviction that all sorts and conditions of men flocked to hear him.

By and by rumors of the preaching of this great prophet reached the ears of Herod. He became curious to see him. In spite of the fact that he had given rein to every lust, he was a bit bored. Maybe this strange man would bring him a new thrill. Then, maybe Herod was heart-hungry. Maybe even in his petty soul there was a lingering longing for a better life. Why not give him credit for this? Hunger for goodness and for God belongs not to the saints alone, but to the sinners as well. Such hunger is universal. Others just as bad as Herod have felt such longings. Yes, and have had them satisfied too. Maybe Herod had a sly, unconfessed yearning for help. But whether from curiosity or heart-hunger, or both, these two, John and Herod, one day faced each other. I have an idea Herod invited John to his palace. He did not wish to join the rabble to listen to the prophet. Therefore he arranged for himself and his paramour to hear John alone.

It was a great hour for these two pampered sinners when they stood face to face with this wilderness preacher. It was an hour that might have changed and remade them. It was also an hour of testing for John himself. How did John meet it? He met it with the fine sincerity and courage that had characterized him as a wilderness preacher. Here he did not rebuke the sins of society in general. He came to grips with the ugly cancer that was gnawing at the vitals of Herod and Herodias. It takes no great courage, generally speaking, to preach plainly to a multitude. But to deal faithfully with those who have power to make or to break you, that requires courage of the highest type. That is what John did. He passed for the present over the other nine commandments and dealt with the seventh, the sin of adultery. This man was living with a woman who was not his wife, and this woman was living with a man who was not her husband. John made them face that fact.

Not only so, but he made his rebuke in the most courageous fashion. He might have softened the blow by saying, "You are among a fanatically religious people. They believe strongly in the sacredness of the marriage tie. For you two to disregard it is bad politics. Your conduct, therefore, is not expedient. You would be more popular, you would have less trouble with your subjects, if you would have more regard for their convictions." But he based his plea on the bedrock principle of right and wrong. "In living as you are living," he said, "you are sinning against the fundamental rightness of things. It is not lawful for thee to have thy brother's wife." It took courage to say that.

As Herodias listened her keen, cruel eyes opened wide in amazement. Her face became tense and white with anger. She made up her mind then and there that this bold prophet should pay for those words with his life. She did not get angry with the disease from which she was dying. Instead she only got angry at the physician. But Herod with all his baseness was not quite that low. He, too, listened with amazed resentment. The sermon perhaps made him for a brief period very uncomfortable. Its plain bluntness shocked him. But in spite of this, there was that in the sermon that made a tremendous appeal. The story says that Herod heard John gladly.

That fact takes us by surprise. Few of us like to be told plainly of our own sins. But Herod seems to be an exception. Why was this the case? I think Herod got a bit of a thrill out of meeting somebody that was brave enough to tell him the truth. He had been fawned upon and flattered all his life. His friends had lied to him openly and to the point of nausea. Here at last was one that looked him in the eye and told him the ugly truth about himself. Naturally it shocked him, yet he could not bring himself wholeheartedly to resent it. It was something new to face the facts about himself, even though it made him uncomfortable. It was something new also to face a man good enough, big enough, and brave enough to tell him the truth, even though he might have to pay for such truth-telling with his life. But, be the reasons what they may, the sluggish soul of Herod was thrilled by John and by his preaching.

But Herod did more than thrill at the message of John. He took that message seriously. Under John's preaching, Herod's conscience, after suffering long from sleeping sickness, began to awake. He determined to make some improvements in his rotten life. The story says that he did many things. He doubtless vowed that he would leave off some of his evil practices. At least one of the many things that he did was to resolve that he would not be so quick to shed innocent blood. Hence he began by protecting the life of the prophet who had rebuked him. Herodias was for putting John to death then and there. But Herod would not stand for it. There were still some crimes that even this cruel fox refused to commit.

But though Herod did many things under the preaching of John, he did not do the supreme thing. That was his tragedy. He spent his time tampering with the outside of his life instead of having it set right at the center. He saw that his clock was not running right. Therefore he sought to polish the hands. But he did nothing for the inside. A lovely spring on our farm once became so stenchful that even the horses would not drink from it. We found that an animal had died at its very source. No amount of cleaning and cultivation of the environs of that spring would help. The corruption had to be taken out of its heart. Herod was deeply stirred, but he was not stirred enough to repent. This left him ripe for his continued downward course.

III

One of Herod's most fatal steps downward grew out of his birthday celebration. This foxy man was to have a birthday. Now in those primitive days even intelligent people knew of no better way of celebrating a birthday than to throw a wild party. They thought that the prize way to have a good time was for everybody to get drunk. Of course we have learned far better in these enlightened days. But we must remember that we are here dealing with a rather primitive people. Drink was passed in abundance and all the guests were verging on drunkenness. Now Herodias was keeping an eye on the scene. She had a plan for the satisfaction of her lust for revenge. When she saw that Herod was drunk enough to be a bit of a fool she sent her daughter in to perform a salacious dance. This dance appealed to lustful Herod. When she had finished, his enthusiasm knew no bounds. He promised the dancer with an oath that he would grant any request she would make, even to the half of his kingdom. Having received that promise, this daughter hurries to her mother, who instructs her as to the request she is to make. "Give me," she said, "the head of John the Baptist in a dish."

That grim request half sobered Herod. Corrupt and drunken fool that he is, he does not wish to commit this crime. But he has taken an oath. He has made a vow. He must keep his word. Is it ever right to lie? Is it ever right to break a vow that we have taken? Certainly. There are some vows that are far more honored in the breach than in the keeping. I once knew a mother whose daughter brought shame upon her home. This mother solemnly vowed that the daughter should never cross the threshold of that home again. She made it in solemn earnestness. For months she kept it. But by and by she broke it. I was there at the breaking of it, and the peace of heaven came back in that mother's face as a result of breaking that horrible promise. Herod should have broken his vow.

But more binding upon him than his vow was the crowd in which he found himself. "For the sake of them that sat with him," says the story, "he commanded it to be given her." We choose our friends and those friends help to make us or break us. You can choose such friends for yourself that life at its best will be far easier for you. You can also choose such friends as to make right living for you next to impossible. I read a letter sometime ago written by a young chap just before he took his own life. "Bad company," he said, "has been my ruin. I ran with the wrong crowd." Herod, feeling bound by his oath and urged on by this cruel crowd, sent an order for the Prophet's execution. A little later Herodias was gloating over the head of John the Baptist, and that at the very table where John might have feasted had he been more a coward and less a hero.

IV

This brings us to the final scene in Herod's life. His awakening by John was to little purpose, for soon he fell asleep again. But even yet his conscience was not entirely dead. Another peasant Preacher was abroad, and the nation was being stirred to its depths. On everybody's lips was the question as to who this new Prophet was. Some said that he was Elijah, while others said that he was one of the old prophets come back to life. But Herod was sure as to the Prophet's identity. "This," he declared, "is John the Baptist whom I beheaded." There seems hope for Herod even yet. I doubt if he ever acknowledged this crime before. He had probably blamed it on Herodias or on the crowd. But now in the light of these reports about Jesus he stands alone and face to face with his crime. He acknowledges that bloody deed as his very own.

But this awakening on the part of Herod was very brief. Though still interested in Jesus, his interest was born of antagonism rather than of friendliness. Then his antagonism died and he became merely curious. He was still eager to see Jesus, but with no thought of being helped by him. His one hope was that Jesus might give him a momentary thrill by performing some miracle. Herod had his chance at last when the Master was standing under the very shadow of the cross. When the Jews routed Pilate out of bed early that fateful Friday morning and demanded that he try the Master, Pilate did his best to dodge the issue. Learning that Jesus was from Galilee, he hustled him off to Herod. The Fox was gleeful. He began at once to ask Jesus many questions. These questions had been piling up for months. And what answer did Jesus make? He answered never a word, not a single syllable.

That I take it was most startling and amazing. Why, I wonder, was this the case? It was certainly not because Jesus was angry at Herod. It was not because he has lost all patience with him. It was not because he had ceased to love him. He loves all, good and bad, with an everlasting love. He did not speak to Herod because he knew that to speak would do no good. This fox had trifled with the truth till his ears had become stopped. He had shut his eyes to the light till his eyes had gone out. There is sound psychology in that solemn doctrine of the sin against the Holy Spirit. It does not seem that one may resist the wooings of the Spirit till he can no longer make his voice heard. At least the infinitely loving Christ stood in the presence of Herod and had no single word to say to him.

And how did the interview end? Having found that Jesus would not satisfy his curiosity, in bitter scorn he threw on him an old purple robe and with loud laughter sent him back to Pilate. There is something terrible about that laughter. It sounds as if the hounds of his own unleashing are closing in upon the Fox. But we make a great mistake if we convince ourselves that the case of Herod is unique. However strong our convictions, we may disregard them till they seem like mere trifles. However high and precious our ideals, we may through disloyalty come to scorn them. There is no deeper tragedy than to reach the place where we can laugh at those high values that once brought us with reverence to our knees. H. G. Wells has a frightful story whose horror grows out of the fact that the lighted candles in a certain haunted room go out one by one. Maybe that is the tragedy of some of us. One by one our lights are going out. "Let him that thinketh he standeth take heed lest he fall."

19
The Fatal Refusal

He went away (Mark 10:22).

"He went away." This short sentence contains the tragedy of a soul. You cannot read it intelligently without feeling a touch of heartache. It makes you lonely like sitting by a fireside that is cold, waiting for steps that never come. "He went away." Not that Jesus put his two hands on his shoulders, turned him about, and pushed him away. Not that Jesus looked into his soul and saw stains that made discipleship for him an impossibility. Not that he read his yesterday and told him that its soiled pages made it impossible for him to accompany Him. "He went away." This young man, holding his destiny in his own hands, having the power to say yes or no, turned his back on the wooing, winsome Christ and refused to follow Him.

His story is one of the most disappointing to be found in the New Testament. This is true because we know of no single man that came into personal contact with Jesus during his earthly ministry who was richer in possibilities. No story of any disciple begins more hopefully than does the story of this man. No morning ever had a more promising dawn than his. Therefore it is all the more sad when we see this bright morning change into gloom and tempest and night. One moment he is running courageously to meet Jesus. He is even kneeling at the feet of Jesus. The next he has gone away, carrying with him his fine gifts and his big, broken heart. How disappointing! The superb worth of him only makes his failure the more tearful and pathetic.

I

Look what tremendous assets he brings to this interview.

A. There is the wealth indicated by the name that he has come to wear. He is the "Rich Young Ruler." Material wealth is in his hands. That means power. Money is condensed energy, it is pent up force. If consecrated to God, it may be an instrument of endless good. Then, he is a ruler. That is, he belongs to the aristocracy. He is a "blue blood." He is a member of that class that was later to crucify Jesus. How much he might have done to win those of his social standing if he had only given himself up to the Master.

Better still, he is young. He is standing at the morningtide of life. It is fine to surrender to Jesus at any time. It is great to be born again even if that wonderful transformation takes place when we are old. It is better to give the last brief inch of life's dying candle to Christ than never to surrender at all. But how much better it is to give Him a whole life! He was young. His was the privilege, therefore, of giving himself to Jesus from the sweet days of springtime to the last hour of winter. That privilege is a treasure unspeakably rich. Christ wants your old age, but how intensely He yearns for our youth.

B. Then this young man was possessed of a noble restlessness. He was in the grip of a fine discontent. Now, there is much of our discontent that is mean and unworthy. This is usually the case when we are dissatisfied only with what we have. Such dissatisfaction is, as a rule, not a mark of bigness, but of littleness. It is not a mark of unselfishness, but of the opposite. Here are two babies. They each have a rattle. Those rattles are exactly alike. But one sees that in the hands of the other. He throws his own away and seeks to possess that of his neighbor. This they do because they are babies.

This young man was not simply dissatisfied with what he had. Of course he had discovered that things were powerless to meet his deepest needs. But his supreme discontent was with himself. He was not restless because of what he possessed. He was restless because of what he was. Though rich in the things that almost all desire, he knew that he had not attained the best. He was looking wistfully toward the heights.

Now it is for such a man that we can hope. The self-satisfied man drives us to despair. If you are as learned as you want to be, you are not likely to learn any more. If you are as good as you want to be, you will certainly not get any better. If you are as high up the hill as you care to be, then you will not climb any higher. Self-satisfaction stops us on the road of life. It means arrested development. But dissatisfaction opens the way to progress.

Some years ago, a brother and myself were summering in Colorado Springs. While students at Webb School, we had heard Mr. Webb tell of a visit he had once made to the top of Pike's Peak. There was no cog road running up the mountain at the time of his visit. To reach the summit, those who did not walk had to ride either on burrors or in carriages. He declared, therefore, that he exercised great care in selecting his conveyance. He wanted to be sure of reaching his destination. At last he chose a carriage with these words written on its sides: "Pike's Peak or bust." He believed that this motto went far toward guaranteeing success.

Now on the very day after our arrival we decided to visit Pike's Peak. But we made no effort to locate the carriage that Mr. Webb had used. No more did we choose a burro. We even scorned the motor car. We determined to climb. We entered upon this undertaking, however, with the motto in our hearts and upon our lips that we had learned from our famous teacher. "Pike's Peak or bust," we said glibly as we set out upon our journey. Soon we found that the undertaking was far more difficult than we had expected. How endless the road seemed. How weary we became. But when I would drop behind, my brother would shout back at me, "Pike's Peak or bust." Then I would put forth extra energy till I found myself in the lead. Then I would call back to him that same ringing battle cry, "Pike's Peak or bust." How near it came to being this latter you will never know. But we refused to give up.

Here and there, however, we would stop and take a view of the way along which we had come. We would gaze with delight upon the far-flung panorama that lay below. There at the foot of the mountain was the little village of Manitou; a little further away, Colorado City, then Colorado Springs. Stretching far in the distance was the wistful plain. As we looked and thrilled we said, "This is enough for today, let us go back and come again." Then we would turn our faces and there, far above us, we could glimpse the summit, scintillating and sparkling under its mantle of eternal whiteness. It seemed to be calling to us, "You have not seen the highest yet; the best is yet to come." And we could not rest until we had reached the top.

This young man was being lured by the heights. That was the secret of his restlessness. Had he responded, he would have found his needs abundantly met. For walking with Christ is like making a journey into a new country. It is like a mountain climb where the atmosphere becomes more bracing and where the panoramas become more enchanting with each step of the way. Happy is the man whose spiritual hungers and thirsts make him dissatisfied. Happy is he whose dissatisfaction sends him to Him who is able to satisfy the longing soul and to satisfy it forevermore.

C. Not only was this young man possessed of a noble restlessness but he was an eager seeker after that which could give him rest. How earnest he was. How enthusiastic. We read that he ran to find Jesus. Enthusiasm is beautiful in any worthy cause. Everybody loves earnestness just as everybody hates insipidity and negativeness. But if enthusiasm is commendable in the ordinary affairs of life, how doubly commendable is it in the pursuit of the highest and of the best. How tragic to be enthusiastic and dead in earnest about the things of secondary value and listless and indifferent about the things of eternal value. This young man was an earnest and enthusiastic seeker after Christ.

D. He was a man of great courage. He ran down the road to find Jesus when nobody else was running. That in itself was a very courageous piece of conduct. It is easy to run with a crowd. But how hard when you run alone. It is easy to stand with the multitude but it is not easy to stand alone. Then of the few that were about Jesus, not one was in his social circle. They were not aristocrats, that little handful of fishermen. The Master Himself was not. What fine courage it took, therefore, for this "blue blood" to go down the road before the gaze of the crowd and get down on his knees before a man who had the calloused palms of a day laborer.

E. Then this young man was reverent. This is a fine virtue that is none too common. A present day humorist has declared that if you were to examine the bump of reverence on the head of the modern man you would find it to be a dent. Reverence is a mark of moral fineness. It is the roadway to knowledge in every department of life. It is absolutely essential if we are to make our way into the secret place of the Most High. This young man in spite of culture and wealth and position still knew how to bend the knee. He still knew how to pray. He was reverent.

F. Finally, he was morally clean. He was beautifully unspotted. He was loyally religious. When Jesus put to him the moral law he was able to answer, "All this have I observed from my youth." Think not that he was falsifying. Think not that he was playing the hypocrite. Jesus who saw into the heart of him did not think so. Had he thought so He would have rebuked him. But He did not rebuke him. He accepted his statement for what it was, the plain truth. He appreciated his fine moral worth and gave him high approval.

"Then Jesus, beholding him, loved him." Then Jesus, looking at him searchingly and seeing how manly and straightforward and clean he was, loved him. Do not stumble at the fact that Jesus had a peculiar love for this man. Do not think for a moment that because He is the Saviour of the world He looks with the same eyes upon the pure and upon the vicious. Do not think for a moment that He looks with the same eyes upon the young fellow that is clean and upon him that is a moral leper. As far from perfection as we are, we do not. Christ loves all with an everlasting love. But He looks with peculiar love upon those possessed of the high moral worth that belonged to this young man.

II

But in spite of all these fine assets, there was a want in this young man's life. He acknowledged as much when he came to kneel at the feet of the Master. When Matthew tells the story, he puts this question in the young man's mouth, "What lack I yet?" "I have wealth and position. I have decency and morality. I am even religious. Yet there is a want in my life. I have missed the highest. I have not found the best. What is the matter?" To this statement of the case Jesus agreed exactly. He did not tell the young man that he was a bit morbid. He did not say that he was unfair in his judgment of himself. He said, "One thing thou lackest." "With all of your fine qualities, with all of your splendid virtues you have not arrived. There is something wanting." "One thing thou lackest."

A. What was the thing that this young man lacked? I stood beside a baby bed the other day in which a little girl was suffering. By and by, I saw her lift her hand and strike a curl of golden hair that lay upon her forehead and then drop that hand at her side. I heard the mother sob. I saw the face of the father become wet with tears. What was the matter? As I looked at that little girl her hair was just as golden as it ever was. Her teeth were just as pearly white. Her little hands were just as delicate and shapely. Yet I had to say, "Bessie, darling, one thing thou lackest." What was it? Life. The sweet little girl was dead.

What was the matter with this Rich Young Ruler? What did he lack? Answer, he was short on spiritual life. He was religious. But his religion was not that essential something that means the life of God in the soul. He was a member of the Church, but he had not been born anew. He was moral, but had never passed out of death into life. He had a thousand good qualities, but he had never laid hold on Him who came that we might have life and have it in abundance.

But, there he is kneeling at the feet of Him who is a Specialist in the realm of Life. He is kneeling before Him of whom it is said, "He that hath the Son, hath Life and he that hath not the Son hath not Life." And this Jesus is telling him the way out of his want. He is telling him how the one thing he lacks may be possessed in rich abundance. He makes it very plain. "Go thy way, sell whatsoever thou hast and give to the poor,—and come, take up the Cross and follow me." And what response does he make? Does he spring to his feet in gladness? Does he burst into thanksgiving that the way has been made so plain? By no means. He rises with night in his soul and a sob in his throat and turns away.

B. This brings us therefore to his second lack. Not only did he lack Life, but he lacked the willingness to pay the price of Life. Jesus read the heart of him. He knew what stood in his way. He knows what stands in your way and mine. It may be a trifle. It may be something that is very wonderful. But whatever it is, if it keeps you from saying, "Yes" to Jesus Christ, then it has proved your undoing. The Young Ruler wanted to be a Christian, but he did not want to be one intensely enough to pay the price. Therefore, he went away.

III

What was the result of his refusal?

A. First, he failed to become a disciple of Jesus. That was true in spite of all his fine qualities. That was true in spite of this fact that Jesus yearned to number him among His friends and followers. Does not the story say that He loved him? But even He cannot compel the weakest of us to follow against his will. All He can do for this fine young man is to invite him. If he refuses, if he goes away, then there is nothing more than He can do. He did go away. He refused to follow Jesus. Therefore he missed the high privilege of becoming a disciple.

B. Refusing to become a disciple, he refused Life. What a tragedy! Refusing Life, he refused all that could satisfy either in this world that now is or in that which is to come. Look! He is going away. Where? Back to his wealth, back to his palace, back to his possessions. But these had not met his needs before. They were still more powerless to meet them now. Where is he going? Away from Life. Now the road away from Life leads only toward death. So the last glimpse we get of this princely young man, he is facing toward abiding restlessness, moral poverty, spiritual death.

"He went away." That is a sentence out of the biography of a man who lived and fought and lost long years ago. Tonight you face the same Christ that he faced. He had his chance and threw it away. You still have yours.

The Christ that yearned for him, now yearns for you. The Christ that invited him, now invites you. Your response to that invitation remains yet to be written. What answer will you make? "Will you also go away?" asks the Master wistfully. Will you not answer in the language of one who loved Him well enough to die for Him—"To whom shall we go but unto Thee? Thou hast the words of eternal life!"

20

The Frozen Face—Lot's Wife

But his wife looked back from behind him, and she became a pillar of salt (Gen. 19:26).

Here is a striking story that is very modern and up to date. But we of today often miss it because of the queer costume in which it is dressed. Here is a woman warned to flee from a doomed city. She is further warned that she is not once to look back. She must keep her face toward the heights. At last she gives her consent and begins the journey. But she disregards this latter warning. She has lived in Sodom for a score of years. Naturally it has some delightful associations. It has some haunting memories. She cannot break with it all at once. Therefore, she takes one lingering backward look. The result is disaster. She becomes a pillar of salt.

How queer it all sounds! Not only is it queer, but it seems to smack of the absurd. What a travesty on a loving God to think that he would punish in this drastic fashion such an innocent something as a backward look. Certainly this old folk story must have been written by one who knew little of either God or man.

But let us not reach this conclusion too quickly. Here is an arresting fact. Jesus read this old story. He looked at this frozen face with its sightless eyes turned back toward Sodom. He read in it not an absurd slander against the love of God. He read in it rather a solemn warning to the men of his day and to those of ours. As he pauses at our side to gaze at this strange figure, he says to us, solemnly, almost sternly, "Remember Lot's wife."

I

Look at the background of this story. A good many years before, Abraham and Lot had left Ur of the Chaldees to journey into the unknown. Abraham believed that he was making this adventure at the call of God. Lot had caught something of the contagion of his faith and enthusiasm and had joined him. For years nothing came of Abraham's mad dream. That is, there was no heir; no son was born to be the father of many nations. But both Abraham and Lot prospered materially. Their immense prosperity brought on strife, and they decided that it would be wise to separate. In fulfillment of this plan they take their stand, I imagine, on a promontory that gives a lookout on all the surrounding country. Then Abraham with fine generosity gives the younger man first choice.

Lot, with an eye for the main chance, begins to look in every direction. Over to the right is a wild rugged country. Here the grass is not luxurious, but the herdsmen can find sustenance for their flocks if they keep moving. But over in the other direction is a marvelously beautiful country. The story says that it looked like the garden of the Lord. As Lot looks on the landscape as the oriental sunlight kisses the dewdrops on the lips of the grasses into a million jewels, he smiles. The scene makes his palms itch. "If I go that way," he says to himself, "I will get on. I will make a pile of money." But even as he looks his smile changes into a frown. What is the matter? He sees the cities of the plain, Sodom and Gomorrah. To him, they are as cesspools in a flower garden, as horrid blemishes on an otherwise lovely face. Thus the scene repels while it appeals.

As he looks in the other direction, he says to himself, "If I go this way I will not make so much money, but I will have a better chance at the values that last. I will have a better chance at God. My children will have a better chance at God. My wife, who is a bit worldly, will have a better chance at God." Thus he stands, making up his mind. That way a better chance at things, this way a better chance at God. It is a choice we have to make and make every day. Which way did Lot go? Here is the tragic answer. "He pitched his tent in the direction of Sodom." He made a wrong choice, and that wrong choice led him in a wrong direction.

Now as he was going in a wrong direction we are not surprised that he reached a wrong goal. We read in the very next chapter after this incident that Lot dwelt in Sodom. That was not his goal when he set out. He was only going in that direction. But little by little he came closer to Sodom till he moved into the city. Then in the chapter of which our text is a part we read that Lot sat in the gate at Sodom. Not only had he moved into Sodom, but he had become mayor of the city. I can well guess the platform on which he ran. He was going to give the city a business administration. That is what every city wants. That is what few cities get. So for a score of years Lot lived and prospered in Sodom. These years might have been years of moral enrichment to Lot and his family and to Sodom as well had he been true to his faith. But he did not change Sodom; Sodom changed him. That is ever the case. If we do not try to change our world for the better, it will change us for the worse. Sodom became for Lot and his wife more than a point on the map. It became an attitude of Godless worldliness.

Then one day heavy news came their way. They were informed that Sodom was going to be destroyed for its wickedness. Of course, that message was in no sense unique. All that was unique about it was that it came in a dramatic fashion, and was carried out in a spectacular and dramatic way. But that same doom is being pronounced again and again. "The soul that sinneth, it shall die." It is pronounced against every Godless city, and against every Godless nation. This sentence, then, that sounds queer and harsh is the language of the whole Bible. It is the language of human history. Our graveyards are littered with nations that have died of their own sin. Sodom then became what Bunyan would call "The City of Destruction."

But while the city was doomed, Lot and his wife were offered an opportunity to escape. They were given the privilege of beginning life anew in the clean atmosphere of the hills. Life in Sodom had been disappointing to both of them in spite of their love for it. They had never been able to forget the faith that had once been theirs. Once along with Abraham they had builded altars. Once they had looked to the heights. Once they knew how to pray. They had been homesick for this better life many times. They had been pained and disgusted by the wickedness of Sodom many times. We read of Lot that they vexed his righteous soul from day to day. And now at last there was a chance for them to escape it all and begin life anew. But they looked at their opportunity with cold and critical eyes. They felt as if God were trying to cheat them out of something. "You must begin life anew," said God's messenger. But their faces did not light up. "Do we have to?" they asked gloomily. "You must be born anew," said Jesus centuries later. And we look at him with reluctant faces and say, "Must we?" forgetting that this "must" is not one of compulsion, but of highest possible privilege.

Not only did these two regard the privilege of beginning anew without enthusiasm; they resolved to postpone acting upon it as long as possible. "Of course," they said, "we must leave Sodom with its moral decay, with its rapidly approaching doom, sometime. Sometime we must go toward the heights. But let us postpone it as long as possible."

Do not be impatient with them. Do not sneer at them. We have acted with the same blindness a thousand times, and with far more light than they had. How many there are who expect to be Christian someday, but desire to put off the hard ordeal as long as possible. They virtually say, "Let me live for myself; let me live apart from God; let me cheat myself of life abundant as long as possible. Let me rob myself of my highest usefulness as long as possible. I want to be a Christian someday, but my motive is not that I might be and do my best. It is only that I might escape the doom of Sodom."

Having postponed their decision till they felt that death was close upon their tracks, Lot and his wife at last turned their backs upon Sodom and made a reluctant start for the hills. But there was no eagerness in their going, no high enthusiasm. This was true of Lot, but it was even more true of Mrs. Lot. The story says, "She looked back from behind him." That is significant. Feeling the strong tug of Sodom upon her soul, seeing no compelling beauty in the heights, she did not make much progress. She traveled with slow and reluctant feet. Soon even tortoise-like Lot had outstripped her. She found herself cut off from the group. She said, "I will just take one last look in spite of the fact that such a look is forbidden." She so turned, and the volcanic ashes embalmed her. And there she stood a grotesque statue with her face turned back toward death.

II

What is the meaning of this weird story? Why this tragic doom? Believe me, there was nothing arbitrary about it on God's part. Sometimes we read this story in such a wooden fashion that we fancy that the author is trying to tell us that God struck this woman dead for doing so innocent a thing as looking back to the city where she had lived for a score of years. But this is not the case at all. This woman was not so much punished for her sin as she was punished by her sin. This backward look on her part worked tragedy, I know. It has worked the same tragedy in countless millions of lives. It will work the same tragedy in your life and mine if we give way to it. God is therefore not punishing this woman because he is vindictive and angry.

Nor are we to think of this act of disobedience on the part of Mrs. Lot as one born of sheer stubbornness. She did not reach a certain spot where she planted her feet with grim determination and said, "Beyond this I will never take another step. I have made up my mind that I will neither live in Sodom nor in the heights. From now on I am going to abide exactly where I am." That was not her intention at all. She was going to stop for only a moment. Hers was a temporary pause, as she herself thought. She was a temporary transgressor, even as you and I. No one of us intends to hold on to our sin forever. We are only going to enjoy sin for a season. But that temporary stop became for her, as it may for us, eternal.

What, then, was wrong? It was not the backward look. The backward look was not the disease from which this woman was suffering; it was only a symptom. I knew a young chap some time ago who began to take on extra weight. Getting a bit heavier is no calamity, especially to one who is naturally thin. But it was tragic in the case of this young man. His physician said that his extra weight was a symptom of a deadly disease. This backward look is like the idle word against which Jesus warns. I remember how harsh it seemed to me as a boy that we were to have to give account to God for every idle word. But the idle word is the unguarded word. It is the word that focuses the light upon our souls. It is not the idle word, therefore, that is significant, but the character that the word reveals. Even so this backward look was an indication of a fatal disease of the inner life. It indicated that this woman was suffering from a divided heart.

Here, then, is a word that comes close to every one of us. A divided mind spells tragedy. This is affirmed by the whole Bible. It is most emphatically affirmed by Jesus. There is nothing upon which our Lord insists with greater urgency than the necessity of wholeheartedness. To fail to make up one's mind, to be divided in allegiance is to make discipleship an impossibility. "No man can serve two masters: for either he will hate the one, and love the other; or else he will hold to the one, and despise the other. Ye cannot serve God and mammon." For instance, a young man once came to Jesus all enthusiasm, saying, "Lord, I will follow thee whithersoever thou goest." Do not think for a moment that the heart of Jesus did not warm to that declaration. But as the Master looked at him and read his very soul, he saw that while discipleship made a tremendous appeal, things made a yet greater appeal. Therefore, he gave him this answer: "Foxes have holes, and the birds of the air have nests, but the Son of man hath not where to lay his head." What does Jesus mean? This is not the language of self-pity. The Master is not appealing for sympathy because he is more homeless than the foxes and more destitute than the birds of the air. He is rather emphasizing his own freedom. "I am as free," he declares joyfully, "as these creatures of the wide open spaces. I am not enslaved by things. If you are going to be my disciple, you must be willing to share my independence. You cannot serve God and things."

"Follow me," said Jesus to another friend. That friend had also felt the spell of the Master and was eager to obey. There was but one hindrance. That was his devotion to his father. Therefore this man replied, "Let me first go and bury my father." By this he is not meaning to say that his father is dead. He means this, rather: "My father would be very disappointed and very lonely were I to leave him now to become your disciple. But if you will wait till he is dead, then I will come gladly." But Jesus could not accept any such divided allegiance. Therefore he said, "Let the dead bury the dead; but go thou and preach the kingdom of God."

Then there was a third man who heard the appeal of Jesus and felt his compelling spell. He, too, was perfectly willing to become a disciple, provided he could make his own terms. He was willing to give Jesus any place in his life except first place. Therefore he said, "Let me first go bid them farewell which are at home at my house." "Let me first say good-bye to my people at home," Moffatt translates it. This man had a family. Perhaps he had guests that he felt he could not leave without telling them good-bye. But Jesus answers with solemn earnestness, "No man, having put his hand to the plow, and looking back, is fit for the kingdom." There was no anger in this. It was just a plain statement of fact. A divided mind unfits us for the business of living in every department of life. It makes vital Christianity utterly impossible.

III

But wherein is the divided man an unfit man? What are some of the penalties we pay for being of a divided mind?

A. We miss the joy that is the privilege of the decided. Our most wretched hours are generally hours of indecision. To be unable to decide between two prizes is to experience the pain of missing both. Where did Lot's wife die? She did neither in Sodom nor in the heights. Trying to make the best of both worlds she lost both. I remember a cow we used to have that was fond of jumping fences. She was an awkward creature. She seldom made a really successful jump. Usually she fell upon the fence and hung there. Thus, with her hind feet in one pasture and her fore feet in the other, she would lie and moan, getting nothing out of either pasture. To find real joy in living one must be wholehearted.

B. A divided heart makes us unfit because it robs us of our strength. The strongest of men will accomplish little if he cannot say, "This one thing I do." But an ordinary man can do the impossible if he is a man of one purpose. Listen to this old story again: "His wife looked back from behind." Why had she fallen behind? It was not lack of strength, but a divided will. Never can we travel very swiftly toward the heights if our hearts are in Sodom. If our eyes are looking back to the world, we are not likely to make much progress toward the things of the spirit. A divided heart makes us unfit because it robs us of our joy and of our power to go forward.

C. Finally, indecision ends in disaster. By this I do not mean that disaster always comes in the dramatic fashion in which it came to Lot's wife. We miss the whole point of the story if we think that the tragedy of this woman was her physical death. Her tragedy was not physical, but spiritual. This crude figure with its face turned toward Sodom gives us a photograph of the woman's soul. Sudden death did not turn her face in the wrong direction. The woman herself did the turning. All death did was to freeze that backward looking face so that all the future centuries might see it. Her backward look would have been just as tragic, perhaps even more so, had she lived a hundred years longer.

We read the same lesson in the story of the rich farmer of whom Jesus told. One day while he was congratulating himself on his abundant crops and his well-filled barns, God broke in upon his soliloquy with this harsh word: "Thou fool! this night thy soul shall be required of thee." But why was this man a fool? He was not a fool because death dashed upon him without warning. Had he kept facing in the same direction he would still be a fool, though he had lived for these nineteen centuries. That which made him a fool was the fact that he ignored God. He was an imbecile before death ever came upon the scene. Therefore, all that death did for him was to freeze that imbecile look upon his face that all might see.

This same truth is enforced by this story: When Pompeii was being excavated there was found a body that had been embalmed by the ashes of Vesuvius. It was that of a woman. Her feet were turned toward the city gate, but her face was turned backward toward something that lay just beyond her outstretched hands. The prize for which those frozen fingers were reaching was a bag of pearls. Maybe she herself had dropped them as she was fleeing for her life. Maybe she had found them where they had been dropped by another. But, be that as it may, though death was hard at her heels, and life was beckoning to her beyond the city gates, she could not shake off their spell. She had turned to pick them up, with death as her reward. But it was not the eruption of Vesuvius that made her love pearls more than life. It only froze her in this attitude of greed.

Let us, then, listen once more to these solemn words of our

Lord: "Remember Lot's wife." Remember that a wrong choice led to a wrong character. Remember that God gave her a chance to make a new start. Remember that though she took that chance, she took it halfheartedly. Remember that hers was the tragedy of a divided mind. For almost to do a thing is not to do it at all. Almost to be a disciple is to miss knowing Jesus. Almost to be saved is to be lost. Almost to live is to die. Almost to journey to the heights is to share the fate of Sodom just as really as if we never set a foot outside her gates. "How long go ye limping between the two sides? if Jehovah be God, follow him."

Fry, 008